Sticky Fingers'
Vegan Sweets

Sticky Fingers'

Vegan Sweets

100 Super-Secret Vegan Recipes

Doron Petersan

AVERY   an imprint of Penguin Random House   New York

AVERY
an imprint of Penguin Random House LLC
375 Hudson Street
New York, New York 10014

Most Avery books are available at special quantity discounts for bulk purchase for
sales promotions, premiums, fund-raising, and educational needs. Special books
or book excerpts also can be created to fit specific needs. For details,
write SpecialMarkets@penguinrandomhouse.com.

The Library of Congress has catalogued the hardcover edition as follows:

Petersan, Doron.
Sticky fingers' sweets : 100 super-secret vegan recipes / Doron Petersan.
p.   cm.
ISBN 978-1-58333-463-8
1. Vegan cooking.   2. Pastry.   3. Baking.   I. Title.
TX837.P5134   2012   2011047063
641.5'636—dc23

ISBN 978-1-58333-511-6 (paperback)

Printed in the United States of America
1   3   5   7   9   10   8   6   4   2

BOOK DESIGN BY NICOLE LAROCHE

For Peter and Ezra, my two favorite foodies

Contents

Foreword

The first time I walked into Sticky Fingers, I made a scene. A big one. Tucked into a little basement storefront in Washington, DC, was an entirely vegan bakery. I knew ahead of time what I was walking into, which is exactly why I sought out Sticky Fingers. But nonetheless, I found myself screaming and carrying on like a crazy person. In a case before me were rows and rows of insanely exciting and indulgent confections. And I simply couldn't handle it. (That was all before I'd even laid eyes on the soft-serve machine.) Can you even imagine how loud things got once I actually started eating everything? It was mayhem.

It was sometime around 2003, but I still remember it clearly. I got the soft-serve, obvs, a Cowvin cookie, a Little Devil, a Sticky Bun, and one of every cupcake and cookie they had. In a word: sublime. Seriously, every bite was euphoric. And it's only gotten better. Since that day, Sticky Fingers has grown—they moved to a bigger location, went global, and expanded their menu to include all sorts of vegan madness.

I graduated from the University of Maryland, so I have friends in the Maryland-Washington, DC, area. I love them dearly and I visit them once a year. But even if they moved, I'd still need to go back to DC regularly for my Sticky Fingers fix. Doron Petersan has made an addict out of me (along with every other one of her customers).

She's a girl after my own heart. Motivated by her compassion for animals and love for food, she created replicas of all the must-have desserts—the same desserts I loved before my own vegan conversion. When I met her for the first time, I think I did something dorky, maybe bowed to her or groveled on my knees at her feet. I was just so thankful that someone took the time and energy to learn how to make such amazing sweets, all without contributing to the confinement, torture, and slaughter of animals. Vegans are as food-obsessed as the next guy (actually much more so, in my experience); we just don't want cows and hens exploited for their milk and eggs. Doron gets this, and makes it easy for all us vegan gluttons to stuff ourselves silly. She also gets that non-vegans like dessert, too, and she pleases their palates as well. Every single one of her desserts proves that veganism leaves zero to be desired. And it's high time the world gets the message.

When I found out that a vegan had won the second season of *Cupcake Wars*, I made a scene, of course. I was over the moon that for the second time, the winner was part of my tribe—team vegan going two for two on national television! And I was beyond excited that it was Doron, the swami of Sticky Fingers. For years, her passion and dedication have been celebrated by everyone who has set foot in her bakery. Now, with this book, you don't have to be in DC to experience the magic of Sticky Fingers. And if you need to make a scene, you can do so in the privacy of your own home.

—*Rory Freedman, coauthor of* **Skinny Bitch**

Introduction

There are tons of cookbooks out there today claiming to be extraordinary. And vegan baking books? Who can keep up? Fancy titles tout recipes "as good as the real thing, really!" or feature "cardboard-free flavor, promise!" Is that appetizing? "Tested for a year in my own kitchen," claims one author. Is that all ya got? I bet your mom thinks you're the best baker out there, too, and the smartest. Here is the good news: This book is different. You're about to discover the clarity and simplicity of my bakery's very own delectable (if I do say so myself), tried-and-true secret recipes. All the recipes here have been tested and proven delicious by our devoted clientele for more than ten years. Our customers love them, and so will you.

I started Sticky Fingers Bakery in 1999. My days consisted of testing, tasting, selling, making, improving, and then selling some more. Once the hungry vegans of Washington, DC, got word of a new sweets pusher in town, things picked up fast. A generous friend offered a micro loan to get the dough ball rolling. I found a friend who could help bake and a business partner to share the load, and voilà! Our first store, a tiny shared basement bakery hidden under a stairwell, opened in 2002.

Great tasting and free from cholesterol, eggs, butter, and milk? People couldn't believe it! They came from miles around to taste for themselves, and they have since been back for more. As a result, we've been lavished with lots of special attention and highlighted on two Food Network travel shows. Before we could actually say "vegan" on air, *Roker on the Road* and *Road Tasted* with the Deen brothers boasted our egg- and dairy-free concoctions. Let's not forget a win on the season two *Cupcake Wars* "Ice House" episode and a return run on their season three Battle of the Champs. What can I say? You can't win 'em all, but we sure did our best and gave the others a run for their money.

Awards, accolades, morning news crews, and taste challenges, a franchise in Seoul, South Korea, boasting multiple locations, and our own local expansion to a space double the size of the first with savories, coffees, and hot foods to boot! People like us! And it isn't only the vegan kids, either. We are the local bakery that happens to be vegan.

Baking is hard work. It takes much more than passion and love to get a risky business off the ground. And a vegan bakery, total shot in the dark. After years of baking and cake making, sweets pushing and cookie doping, the business partner decided to become a rock star (no lie), the baker friend has been long gone, and the micro loan has been paid off in full. I'm back in the control room running the ship, but hardly doing it solo. With Ben Adams, Jenny Webb, and Kamber Sherrod as the creative team and some twenty other employees on any given day, it takes a village to raise this baby. We have big plans, big dreams, but first we need to make sure everyone is well fed. You can't build an empire if everyone is starving to death or left wanting, now can you?

It's a fact that I refuse to sell anything I won't eat myself. I love food. And I'm vegan. That is how I approach every recipe. Taste and flavor are always the priority, with a dose of simplicity thrown in for good measure (because we all know that if it's difficult to make, we probably won't).

I've separated the chitchat from the recipes so you can easily navigate the most important part, the reason you are here—the food. I love to hear myself talk as much as the next person, but clarity and simplicity are key when baking. If I chat while I cook, I am bound to screw it up, and that would be a tragedy. Cook first, talk second.

I'm a foodie and a nutrition nut who decided that vegan was the way to go. Turns out there are others out there who feel the same way: health-conscious folks craving a sweet fix, animal-ingredient eschewers hoping for a birthday cake, allergic kids looking for an alternative. While I'm not claiming you'll lose a hundred pounds in a week on the all–*Sticky Fingers' Vegan Sweets* diet, chances are that the more you turn to veg alternatives, the further you'll distance yourself from life-threatening ailments.

With many recipes, I've added a little Love Bite, a nutrition-related term of endearment concerning one of the ingredients. They're a healthy incentive. I do concede that everything you are about to make is a treat, and you should act accordingly. There are still calories in these little buggers, and as better for you as they are, they are still feisty little treats and you shouldn't eat the entire batch of cookies in one sitting. Cut the cupcakes with a salad or two. Some steamed veggies, roasted tofu, and wholesome brown rice never hurt, either. But I digress . . .

I vow to bring you recipes that are tasty and healthier without being obvious. Chocolate, sugar, hearty flour, and real flavors and spices are all in the mix. We all know how to make carob-covered frozen bananas and applesauce flaxseed bulgur muffins. You won't find those here.

I've taken our most popular products, scaled them down to a size your kitchen can handle, and attempted to explain the details simply so you can try your hand at the madness. Some are easy, some are tricky, but the more you practice, the better you will get. Baking isn't magic; it's a delicate science that can only be applied if the practice is consistent. It is science. And math. I love math. Grab a beaker and some measuring spoons, put on your specs, and focus. Apply your mad skills.

Chapter 1

The Basics

Weird Science and Lab Lists

Greetings and welcome to the exciting world of Sticky Fingers baking. A pinch of passion, a dollop of curiosity, some sassy scientific practice, a whole lot of risk taking, a ginormous sweet tooth, and voilà! These are the concepts we use most frequently and the sweet treats we sell in our shop in abundance.

Smarts

Traditional baking as we know it is based on a few simple concepts using your standard ingredients: eggs, dairy, flour, leavening, and the sweet stuff. But it's science. Any science-based theory can be broken down, analyzed, and put back together. And that is how we do it. "We" being the bakers and recipe makers, the pioneers here at Sticky Fingers. We know what we want, and in order to get there we tweak the concept and the method to get the same end results as those in the non-vegan baking world. Crèmes and pies? Got it. Cake? You betcha. It works every time, and I am going to show you how. I'm here to dispel the myths that this needs to be difficult, that anything without butter or eggs can't taste good, and that you will suffer for trying to make the world, your body, and your kitchen a better place. This baking might seem a little weird, but it's totally ingenious.

Pay Attention!

As you will see, it's difficult to isolate each reaction and talk about them independently from one another. Well, it's because they don't work that way. They are needy reactions, requiring the support of one another to complete the process. High-maintenance, drama-filled chemical reactions that you get to eat.

It's the nuances and subtleties that will keep your cakes from crumbling and ganache from glopping. Take it from me, a klutzy fast-acting nut with the attention span of a fly. Turn off your phone, the TV, the Twitter, the banter, and pay attention.

Reading Is Fundamental

Do yourself a favor. Read the entire recipe before you get started. Not only do you have to make sure you have all of the ingredients and tools ready, but you have to know what to expect. The only way to do that is to (come on, say it with me) READ THE DIRECTIONS. If you don't follow the order of ingredients, the proper mixing technique, and proper baking time and temp, your dessert doesn't have a chance. There are no microwave instructions in the back of this book. There are no shortcuts in baking. If you want to get the goods, you have to follow the rules. Let's start with the basics, mixing.

The object of mixing is to incorporate and distribute ingredients evenly. Mix too much and you end up with overworked pie crusts, sweet dough that can't be rolled into buns, cakes that won't rise, and cookies that can be sold as paperweights. Cut the mixing short and you end up with grainy textures and partially uncooked products, and not in a good way. Generally speaking, mix until ingredients are evenly incorporated as stated in the recipe, and then stop! A little goes a long way when it comes to mixing batters and dough, and a touch too much can destroy a dessert.

Measure for Good Measure

You can't begin mixing until you get your ingredients together, and that means measuring. This is the end-all be-all, the make or break, the proof of the pudding . . . this is the golden rule of baking: You have to measure accurately and consistently every time. Here at Sticky Fingers, we measure as little as possible. "What the heck do you mean, Doron? That makes no sense." What I mean is that we *weigh* everything above 1 ounce and only use imperial measurements (you know, cups and spoons) for those small, pesky (yet important) "micro" ingredients. Weight is where it's at in baking and where the true consistency lies. You think I'm kidding? Pick up a French pastry or bread book and look at the ingredients. Whether it's metric or imperial, most recipes in the professional cooking world are based on weight rather than measure. The "macro" ingredients, those weighing more than 1 ounce, are weighed because this is the only way to obtain consistency. Taking out the potential variations that come with the heavy handers, flour packers, and sugar spillers is the true way to sweet success. However, with smaller amounts it gets tricky to weigh in the home kitchen. So we've included weights as well as measures for our macro dry ingredients.

Measuring is a technique you can master easily and efficiently. For example, let's focus on flour first to learn how to measure. I'm picking on flour because too much will dry you out and kill your crumb. Too little and your treats will be gummy and gooey. We prefer unbleached and unbromated flours because they are healthier versions of standard white flour, but they can also tend to cause a heavier spread in cakes and muffins. Measuring your flour correctly starts before you pull out a scale or measuring cups. First off, flour should never be stored in a moist or hot environment. Flour can become stale and rancid, leaving a plasticky taste to your intended tasties. Worse, it can clump up, trying to suck all of the moisture from the air. Please place your bag of flour into a sealable plastic bag, or transfer it to an airtight container. If your flour is older than two years (way less for whole grain and fresh milled—more like two or three months), pitch it. You can keep flour in the fridge or freezer to help extend the date, but be sure to bring it to room temp before using. Cold flour does not have the same mixing and binding properties as does room-temperature flour. This is science, remember?

Before you measure, sift your flours:

1. Grab a big metal or glass bowl.
2. Grab a sifter. No, not a colander, a sifter, also known as a fine-mesh sieve.
3. Get your flour. Place the sifter over the bowl and pour some flour into the sifter.
4. Start sifting until you have a big pile of light and fluffy flour.
5. Get a piece of parchment and place your measuring utensils on the paper.
6. Now measure the amount you need from that pile of sifted flour by scooping some out and placing it in your desired measuring utensil. Use a knife to level the flour. Never pack your flour.
7. Pick up that piece of parchment from corner to corner, and dump the rest of the unused flour back into the canister/bag.

Don't lie—you don't want to sift. You are impatient and want to bake as fast as possible. But to skimp and not sift could lead to crumbly and dry baked goods. If you refuse to sift your ingredients, here is what you need to do:

1. Get a piece of parchment paper.
2. Place your measuring utensil on said parchment paper.
3. Spoon flour from the bag or container into your measuring utensil. Overflow it. Note: Do not scoop flour out of the bag or canister using the measuring utensil. This will jam-pack more flour in that cup, causing the flour to be less aerated, the opposite of what we want.
4. With the straight edge of a knife, level the flour by placing the straight side down into the flour, and then push or pull until the flour is perfectly even on the top of your measuring device. This technique should be used to measure *all* of your dry ingredients. Consistency is key, so measure like me.

And remember, do not tap the measuring utensil on your table. This will pack the flour.

Measuring shortening and margarine is a tad easier, especially with those handy-dandy marked wrappers on sticks of margarine and shortening. They sure do make life easy. Simply cut along the desired mark and voilà! But for all of you tub users out there, no worries!

Here's how to measure tub margarine and shortening correctly:
1. Soften the margarine or shortening to room temperature.
2. Using a rubber spatula, scoop your margarine or shortening and press it into your cup or spoon, taking care that you are not leaving any air pockets.
3. Level it off with the straight edge of the spatula. Then scoop it out with that spatula, making sure you get every last fat morsel.

Irreplaceable?

Most people think eggs do all of the work when it comes to baking. But the secret to the egg is in its chemical and nutritional makeup. Eggs provide moisture, as they contain water, saturated fat, and lecithin (an emulsifier that keeps fat and water from separating). And the protein in the egg whites can be used to foam and aerate a batter, provide structure when heated, and, let's not forget, contribute flavor, texture, and color. These are the basic and most common processes in baking. However, eggs are not the only ingredients that contain these magic components or achieve these results. All we have to do to make vegan versions of recipes designed with eggs in mind is to simply re-create the recipe using other ingredients with similar properties. At Sticky Fingers, we look at each recipe and determine what we need to get it to lift, rise, stay soft, and be fluffy. We don't simply think, "What can we use to replace the egg?" but rather "Where are we going and what do we need to get there?" Many people attempt to replace eggs with pureed pumpkin, applesauce, or some other fruit puree, but these types of ingredients don't always work because they don't necessarily do what the egg would have done in that particular baking process. Can you scramble applesauce? Poach pureed pumpkin? Fry fig? Get the gist? Ask yourself, "What am I trying to achieve?" and you are halfway there. Now, let's figure out how to get there. Hidden in the science of mixing, heat, and your common food chemistry are the answers to making recipes without eggs.

Air Supply

The most important and least talked about aspect of mixing has to do with bubbles. Mixing traps air within the mixture, making little pockets throughout your batter and capturing them. Whether it's little soft pockets in cake, the fluffiness of frosting, or tasty sponginess in bread, the concept is the same. We want to make bubbles and capture them in whatever mixture we are making, whether they are tiny bubbles or big ones. That's right, not eggs, but air. We love air. Air is a gas and expands when heated, helping to lift batters and make them light and fluffy. What about water? Water and heat equal steam, which expands when heated. We love steam. Steam is responsible for lots of lift, moisture, and fluff. Getting hot? Mixing causes friction, creating a bit of heat as well. More gas? Carbon dioxide is created when acids react with baking soda and baking powder, also expanding once it is heated, and it gives off a touch of heat as well—see what I'm getting at here? Mixing, temperature, moisture, air, and chemical leavening agents work together to form the structure and texture of your treats.

Vocab Lesson 1

Here are some terms we will use to show you how to mix and when.

FOLDING

Folding is for delicate recipes or when adding in something delicate at the end, like raspberries into cheesecake or oats into cookie batter. We want you to hand mix the ingredients with a spoon or a spatula, turning the bowl with one hand and pulling the mixture into the center of the bowl. This is to keep gluten action to a minimum as well as to prevent delicate ingredients (like raspberries and oats) from falling apart in the batter.

CREAMING

Creaming refers to mixing ingredients so they form a creamy texture. One aspect of creaming is to break down those hard-to-mix ingredients like crystallized sugar. Sugar is creamed with margarine, a nice and soft fat that dissolves the sharp edges of the sugar—but not by too much. The margarine and sugar combine to make a fluffy cream, also capturing some bubbles in there to be used later on in the recipe. We often add vanilla to the creaming process. This is because vanilla is a delicate flavor that needs fat in order to be fully tasted. Vanilla is very aromatic and is more easily smelled than tasted. Try it: Open that bottle and touch a bit to your tongue—not much there to speak of. The vanilla literally holds on to fat molecules and gets carried throughout the recipe. Vanilla is one of the most amazing flavors and one of the most difficult to capture in baking.

WHIPPING

Whipping is the faster, overachieving stepbrother to creaming. You may start off slow to get your ingredients distributed, but you eventually speed things up to incorporate (you guessed it) air. Emulsification is the word for the work here. In Doron-ese, it basically means using something that can get between the fat and the water (opposing elements) and force them together. The cool thing that happens here is that all of this emulsifying makes for serious flavor sensations. Spices, sugar crystals, lecithin, and flour can all emulsify.

INCORPORATING

This means to mix until you can't see clumps or streaks, unless otherwise noted.

CUTTING

This term refers to adding fat into dry ingredients when you want the mixture crumbly rather than fluffy. You can buy a dough cutter that looks like a brass knuckles-style whisk for this purpose. Don't use your fingers, as doing so will melt the margarine or shortening, and remember, our non-hydrogenated margarines and shortenings have lower melting points—they melt at the temperature of your fingers. Do you have a food processor? Use it! With your metal blade, five pulses will perfectly cut the fat.

We Have Chemistry

As Madonna would say, "Physical attraction. It's a chemical reaction." The act of mixing is the physical part. The chemical part happens when baking soda and baking powder act as chemical leaveners and create a chemical reaction where CO_2 is produced. The resulting carbon dioxide can help give more lift to our leavened batters. Remember back in elementary school, when you made that papier-mâché volcano, filled it with baking soda, and then poured the vinegar in? We have taken that bit of elementary knowledge and applied it to most, if not all, of our baked goods. Here in the vegan baking world, we will take all the lift we can get. A little baking soda can go a long way as it reacts with even the tiniest bits of acid. Molasses, cocoa powder (natural), vinegar, and fruit juice all contain acid. However, acid can break down the strength of the protein and starch, so a little acid also goes a long way. Too much can do the same thing that too little can do—nothing.

Baking powder, the other wonder leavener we love so much, is actually made with baking soda. It reacts a little differently because it's already combined with a touch of acid. Once those two hit some liquid, the bubbles begin and the CO_2 does its stuff. The cool thing about double-acting baking powder is that it has power times two. It contains a second type of acid that works its magic when it hits the heat. You get a double rise from double-acting baking powder. Remember, mixing makes heat, so too much mixing can set off the second set of reactions. Another friendly reminder not to overmix your dough and get your goods in the oven ASAP.

Stable Relationships

Now that we have these lovely fluffs of air, we need to trap and stabilize them! Creating cells with gluten or other protein becomes the structure of the ever-coveted crumb.

Gluten is the protein found in flour and many other starchy grains. It is activated by applying moisture and manipulation and is referred to as coagulation or glutenization (gluten action sounds so much nicer). These protein strands are strong (read tough and chewy), so we want to balance that strength with a soft side. This is where the starch from the grain comes in. Starch and liquids combine and actually gelatinize, creating a really smooth texture, great for baked goods. The heat works to cook, or "catch," that protein strand of gluten, and causes the gelatinization process to begin. Some recipes, such as pie and cookie dough recipes, rely more on the gluten action, while others, such as cupcake, muffin, pudding, and curd recipes, utilize more of that starch action. Once the optimal heat is reached, the shape and volume are set. Bake at too low a temp and you risk turning out cakes and puddings that are more like puddles. Bake at too high a temp and you can burn those starches and dry out your protein strands. Fat, sugar, oil, and spices help prevent this, but they can only do so much, as they have other jobs to do.

Fat-astic

There is a reason that fat-free cookies are overly sweet, that fat-free crackers are overly salty, and that fat-free salad dressings are overly sour or bitter. It's because sweet, salty, sour, and bitter are the four flavors your taste buds can easily recognize without the presence of fat. Subtle, aromatic flavors like almond, chocolate, and vanilla don't taste like much when the moisture is removed to make powdery versions or when they are turned into extracts. And without flavor, you have nothing.

Aside from making everything in the world taste better, fat has some work to do when it's used in baking. Most fats have some water content, and that moisture expands when heated, causing the fat to fluff up and help lift and leaven. Straight liquid oil doesn't do much in the fluff department, but it is working hard at carrying around flavors and making everything soft and supple. Those more rigid fats (such as the non-hydrogenated Earth Balance Buttery Spread and Shortening sticks we recommend) will add some air to that fat-moisture combo, getting some gas bubbles going, and giving you even more lifting action. Once the fat starts melting, it spreads throughout the mixture, helping everything not only taste better but feel better, too. Those lovely air pockets we made and stabilized with the starch and protein strands are then coated with the fat as the heat causes it to fluff, rise, melt, and lift. Each "cell" interior will be coated with the yummy stuff, making for a smooth texture in your cookies and cupcakes.

You're Only as Good as Your Machine

Okay, so there isn't really any crazy, fandangled fancy equipment that you need. But there are some things that will make the job easier. Conditional statement: *If you don't have the utensils or equipment I recommend, then we do have alternative solutions for you!* You may get a serious forearm workout, but it will be worth it in the end.

You should always assume each recipe requires measuring utensils and a scale that goes up to five pounds. When measuring liquid you need to have a glass or clear plastic measuring cup. Why? Because I said so, and if I say so, it's for a reason. The reason is when you are measuring liquid you need to get eye level with the liquid to be sure you are on the mark. When working with small batches, it is imperative that you get the measures exact and consistent each time. Why? Because that is how science works.

STEEL

Stainless-steel bowls, utensils, and appliance attachments are the way to go. They hold up under pressure and stay true to form. Unlike plastic and aluminum, you don't have to worry about strong flavors carrying over into your delicate delights.

YOUR KITCHEN CADILLAC

Having a stand mixer is like having an autopilot. For creaming it's imperative and makes life easy. For cookies and sweet dough it does the hard work for you. That said, it is possible to do all of these things without the stand mixer, so keep reading. We have tips for you. It's also easy to overmix and kill your recipes on the stand mixer, so beware.

HAND MIXER

This is the less expensive, more fuel-efficient version of the stand mixer. You can cream, knead dough, or blend any batter with this baby, though it may take a touch longer. Some advice: Use a smaller but taller bowl for creaming so you can get all of the liquids, spreads, and sugars evenly dissolved and properly fluffy. Turn the bowl in one hand while rotating the mixer with the other. Once you have your fluff, then fold in your other ingredients, adding them slowly. It's way easier to mix a little rather than a lot. Take your time!

SCALE

You will need to have a scale that measures up to at least five pounds. (The Ozeri Pro Digital Kitchen Food Scale can be found on Amazon for about $20.) A digital scale with decimals is a must.

Let's say you are going to measure the flour. Put your preferred bowl on top of the scale. If you are using a digital scale, then press zero, or tare, until you see zeros. Then, go ahead and add your flour. Don't forget to choose your unit: If you are measuring for ounces, then use the ounces unit. If you are looking for pounds and ounces, use the pounds/ounces unit. Simple. If you are using a manual scale, be sure to manually zero out your scale once you place the bowl on the platform. All of these scales come with directions, so be sure to stop, focus, and read, please.

WHISK

No whisk? Two forks and some duct tape ought to do it.

OFFSET SPATULA

You'll use this one later in the game for decoration. Imagine your favorite long spatula bent into an L shape near the handle. You *can* use a flat spatula for decorating, but the force of your hand distributes differently. It's more difficult to get an even spread with a flat spatula, so just splurge and get an offset spatula. You will thank me later.

RUBBER SPATULA OR SCRAPER

Get ready to get those fingers sticky. The only way to scrape the bottom of the bowl completely and accurately is with a rubber spatula or bowl scraper. Yes, you may get batter on your hands, but you can use the rubber spatula to scrape the mix off of your fingers and return it to its proper place—no, not your mouth, the bowl. You can lick the bowl after you have your desserts in the oven.

DOUGH CUTTER

This one looks like brass knuckles for baking. It is used to cut your fat and crumb your ingredients so you get the perfect consistency.

SIFTER

I repeat, not a colander, a sifter, also known as a fine-mesh sieve. You can get a fun one with an arm that does the work for you, but a good old-fashioned sifter you bang on your hand works just as well.

SCOOPERS

You know the ones I'm talking about. The ice cream scoopers with the lever you press with your thumb to release the ice cream. They come in a variety of sizes, and they are used for scooping batter and dough to give you a consistent measure. And the handy little lever makes it easier to get the goods out of the scooper. But, most important, you have less contact with the mixture when you use a releasing scoop than you would with a tablespoon or measuring cup. It's quick and easy, so you can get those extra time-sensitive baked goods in the oven faster. Last, you are less likely to remix, and remix again, with a scooper than you would be with a spoon or measuring cup. And you know how much I hate overmixing.

Get an arsenal of sizes. We use our 2-ouncer more than others.

CANDY THERMOMETER

This tool is essential for making caramel if you don't want to learn the details of candying but just want to get to the goods. It's good for your yeast doughs, too. You never want the water to be above 105°F if your yeast is refrigerated or at room temp. But it needs to be at least warmer than the temp of the yeast by 15°F.

MEASURING CUPS

You can't properly measure liquid without glass or clear plastic measuring cups. You need the kind you can see through and that have lines marking the measurements. Stainless-steel measuring cups are preferable to plastic for dry ingredients as well as your margarines and shortenings. They are the easiest to clean after you pack in your fats, and they don't retain odors or flavors.

DISPOSABLE PASTRY BAGS

Disposable pastry bags are hardly disposable at all. We wash them out and reuse them multiple times. You want to make sure you cut them correctly for inserting a tip or for using to drizzle. If you are using a coupler and a tip, place the coupler in the bag to measure how much to cut. Too much and the coupler will squeeze out the end, what we call a blowout. No coupler? Just snip the tip and have at it. No bag? Any plastic storage bag will do. Fill 'er up and clip the corner, enough to let it flow.

OVEN THERMOMETER

Don't trust your oven. After the indicator light goes off, let it heat up ten to fifteen minutes more. Not all oven thermostats are accurate. Other than getting your oven calibrated by a professional, you can use an oven thermometer that hangs from the rack. Place it in front by the window. This is the coolest part of your oven, so once the temp reads to your desired hotness, then you really know it's ready.

Lab List

We recommend certain specific types of ingredients and brands. No kickbacks, no product placement deals, just the ingredients that we have found work best for us. Most of these brand names are not just our preference; the results depend on using them specifically, and changing them will affect the outcome.

FLAVORS

We use extracts or oils, not artificial flavors. Substituting artificial flavors will impart strong, usually chemical fake, flavors. A true foodie will taste the difference. You can use oils and extracts interchangeably by adjusting the amount: Use 1 teaspoon of extract to 1/8 teaspoon of oil. Feel free to add a drop or two more if you like. We recommend using a dropper for measuring your extract or oil rather than pouring it. It's easier and you can add more or less in tiny little amounts.

COCOA POWDER

We use 10 to 12% Dutched cocoa powder. Dutched cocoa is alkalized, versus natural cocoa, which contains naturally occurring acid. Using Dutched allows us to control the acid content using other ingredients. Your recipes may come out a little different if you use natural rather than Dutched cocoa powder: Natural cocoa powder makes for a richer, chocolatier treat. Without the acid, Dutched cocoa can have more of a deep reddish hue and is more easily incorporated into fats and liquids. All recipes here assume you are using Dutched cocoa powder, but feel free to try out natural cocoa powder. It's seriously delicious, though you will have to adjust your recipes a bit. Use 3 tablespoons of natural cocoa powder plus 1/8 teaspoon baking soda to replace 3 tablespoons of Dutched cocoa powder. Or use 3 tablespoons of Dutched cocoa powder plus 1/8 teaspoon lemon juice or vinegar to replace 3 tablespoons natural cocoa powder.

NO FAT-FREE OR LIGHT

The less fat, the less moist and flavorful your products will be. There is a reason all that fat-free stuff in the nineties was crunchy and super-sweet or super-salty. Without fat to help keep the snacks moist, the only flavors that could be tasted were those that didn't need fat or moisture to be able to be tasted. And that would be sweet, salty, sour, and bitter. Fat-free or light coconut milk, soymilk, or margarine just won't work the same as the full-fat stuff, either. Thickeners are added to make the low-fat liquids feel less like watered-down milk and just don't do our baking justice. Trust me, it won't taste nearly as good, and that is the main reason you are here, right? Eating and baking low-fat baked goods is like getting kissed on the cheek and never getting to make out. If you really want a fat-free or lighter alternative, I have two suggestions: 1) eat a smaller portion of the desired dish, or 2) eat fruit.

EARTH BALANCE MARGARINE AND SHORTENING

There are lots of products that claim to be trans-fat-free. Buyer beware—the FDA allows for less than 0.5 gram per serving of trans fats to still be deemed trans-fat-free. There are still trans fats in every bite. It's a common trick of the trade that is used over and over again. How to avoid being tricked? Read the label. If you see "hydrogenated" anything, it contains trans fats. We don't use hydrogenated products in any of our items at Sticky Fingers. We love the vegan Earth Balance Natural Buttery Spread and Sticks to replace butter and margarine and the Natural Shortening sticks for our frosting needs. These are our favorites, but feel free to experiment with other similar non-hydrogenated, natural alternatives to butter and hydrogenated shortenings. Keep in mind that different types of margarines and spreads have different moisture contents and melting points.

TOFUTTI

Tofutti non-dairy non-hydrogenated Better Than Cream Cheese and Sour Supreme: Better Than Sour Cream taste better than any others out there, in our humble opinion. Different binding agents are found in different products and may affect the amount of moisture you need. We love the way Tofutti works for our goodies, and if it ain't broke, don't fix it.

FLOUR POWER

We use unbleached, unbromated all-purpose flour. Better for your bod, better for the environment. You can't replace this with cake flour, bread flour, pastry flour, or whole wheat flour. The recipes won't work; they will either fall apart or be very heavy. Bleached flour is more easy to lift and fluff; unbleached is a little heavier. Even the same types of flours have a lot of variation according to the season, crop, where it comes from, and how old it is. If you find you are coming out with gummy desserts, you can add a touch (1/4 teaspoon) more of your chemical leavener (egg replacer, baking soda or powder) and a teaspoon of lemon juice. This will usually help.

SUGAR BY MANY NAMES

Dehydrated cane juice, evaporated cane sugar, or any mix of the set. It's the sugar we find to be the best of the best. We stick to this one because it's sure to be bone-char free, it's tasty, and it's a smidge better for you than white table sugar. Florida Crystals brand cane sugar is our mainstay in the bakery. This is one ingredient we can be flexible on. While this is our choice brand, everyday plain white granulated sugar will do the trick.

COFFEE

Strong, please. And not decaffeinated. I like my brownies with an extra kick.

Where to Find the Hard to Find

Ingredients, supplies, utensils, and fun decoration stuff can be difficult to find when you first start to look for them. We know where to find them, and once you do, an entire new world of shopping and eating will open up before your eyes.

Most of the ingredients we use can be found at (almost) all Whole Foods, Trader Joe's, local co-ops and natural food stores, and even in most traditional grocery stores. Still can't find them? Try online.

For vegan-specific items, try:

Happy Cow: www.happycow.net. Search the world for vegan ingredients, restaurants, resorts, the whole shebang.

Vegan Essentials: www.veganessentials.com. Super-fun and super-cool stuff. Stop looking at the shoes and go to the food section.

The Vegan Store: www.veganstore.com. One of the first, the pioneers of finding the hard to find.

For other mainstream ingredients that aren't vegan specific but could be hard to find, look to the list below. This is where you can get tons o' good decorating stuff, too. Forget knitting and needlepoint, let baking and decoration be your hobby. You can't eat a scarf, and everyone already has one. But who has a hand-decorated fondant-covered cupcake, hmm?

Kitchen Krafts: www.kitchenkrafts.com. Great for everything from baking ingredients, oils, extracts, food coloring, and decorating supplies! We L-O-V-E Kitchen Krafts.

Chocolate Source: www.chocolatesource.com. I know, right! Who knew you could have this much chocolate delivered to your door?

Sur la table: www.surlatable.com. Everything you want and need in the utensil and supplies department, and some fun ingredients like spices and sprinkles as well. Swank, too.

Target: www.target.com. Affordable supplies and utensils.

Wilton: www.wilton.com. This is where all of us here at Sticky Fingers started. Want to learn to pipe a chicken, pig, or goat? Lattice work to woo any granny? It's here.

Michaels: www.michaels.com. Just about everyone has a Michaels! Great for basics and getting started. If you so much as *look* at Duff frosting or fondants, I will have to take your whisk away.

Remember that skimping on flavorings and spices will cost you in quality and flavor, so splurge on ingredients. You'll thank me later.

Love Bites

Last but most important, these recipes tend to be healthier for you than their non-veg counterparts. Being the nutrition buff that I am, I've included Love Bites, little nutrition tidbits that tout the benefits (some slightly creative) of the ingredients, after many of the recipes. I hope these bites will give you even more of an incentive to try your hand at this baking thing. Nutrition information is vast and plentiful, and I don't want to bore you with entire studies of information, so I grabbed parts and pieces that I think are both interesting and that apply. If you want more information, I can suggest a slew of sources for you. To start, put down the *People* magazine and pick up *VegNews*. You will find fun things to eat and buy, and you won't lose any brain cells. I love me some gossip rags, too, but now is the time for learning so we can get to baking and eating!

Bakers, Start Your Mixers!

Okay, are you ready? You just had a crash course in baking science and learned all of the precious baking secrets we use here at Sticky Fingers. I'm about to show you how it's done. These recipes are the first steps to a long life of Sticky-style baking, the foundation of your dessert future. I want you to take what you are about to learn, hone it, make it yours, and add on. What are you hungry for? What flavors drive you mad? Think about it—you can do it. Let's go!

Chapter 2

Favorite Cakes

Cakes are, hands down, my favorite food. They never miss a birthday and always arrive dressed for the occasion. You can really do a lot with cakes these days (seen any cable lately?), but for now, let's work on the basics. We've broken down the recipes into three categories: chocolate cakes, non-chocolate cakes, and another fun category: boozy cakes! All the chocolate batter recipes use the baking soda acid reaction with CO_2 and steam as the major leaveners. The rest all begin with creaming the margarine and sugar, which is fundamental.

Frostings and Fillings

It's your dirty little secret. Nutritious and healthy by day, secret frosting lover by night. You know who you are, eating the tops of cupcakes first and choosing the corner piece of cake. Frosting in a can never has a chance in your house. Well, it's time to break the hydrogenated habit. Drop that glop! Forget that fake stuff! These frostings are going to save your sweet life.

Refer to pages 7–8 in chapter one where I describe the best techniques for creaming and whipping. You get to control the spread with your frostings. Cream it for luscious and thick versions, whip it good for fluffy and light. Different-size bubbles for different palates. Your creamier frostings will be richer and sweeter with less air in every mouthful. Your whippy versions will taste lighter and less intense, with more time on the mixer making more light bubbles.

The recipes for fillings throughout this chapter are so amazing, so delicious, they will be just as great on the inside as on the outside of your lucky dessert. The trick is in the techniques, which are varied. For example, the caramel and ganache rely on opposite ends of the thermometer to avoid the same candy killer, crystallization. Meanwhile, the curds are so simple they nearly make themselves.

A Note About the Recipes

In this chapter, I've given you a list of our grandest combos, just to get you started. But with all of these recipes, you can also build endless cake creations with all the flavors of your food dreams. I've also given you some guidance if you'd like to use these batters for cupcakes, too. Don't be afraid to embrace your inner (chubby) kid and use your imagination. Pair up old favorites and add on to create new ones. It's your time to shine. Don't be afraid, my sweet maniac. Build! Enjoy! Play!

Before we get into the recipes themselves, let's go over our cake decorating basics.

Cake Decorating

PREPPING

Before we get into frosting techniques, you'll need to prep your cake layers. It is very difficult (and messy) to decorate a freshly baked cake. The starches in the nice little cells you baked up need time to set up and become pliable. Adding the push and pull of a sticky frosting on a new cake can cause cracks and crumbles, and no one wants broken cake (except maybe me, but cake is my favorite food). Once your cake gets to room temperature, you can speed up the process by wrapping the cake in plastic and setting it in the freezer for a bit (about half an hour). Then you'll be in business. (You can also wrap the cake layers in plastic twice and store them in the freezer for up to two weeks. I usually can't wait that long to eat cake . . .)

Once the starches are good to go, you can unwrap your layers and brush any excess crumbs off the tops and sides. Make sure your work surface is free of crumbs as well. (Note: If your cake layers are frozen, bring them to room temperature before frosting them.)

Before you start slinging frosting around, you have to decide how your cake will get to the party. Will you put it on a platter or large plate? Do you have a cardboard or plastic cake board to put it on? It doesn't matter what it is as long as it is at least two inches larger than your cake.

FROSTING TECHNIQUE

If you have a lazy Susan or a turntable, now is the time to get it out. Place a non-slip pad under your cake plate to prevent it from sliding around during the frosting process. If you don't have a lazy Susan or turntable, you'll just need to take things slower and rotate your cake plate with both hands to get the frosting around smoothly. You'll need your offset spatula, a clean, empty bowl for scraping any frosting that has crumbs in it, and a clean towel. Got 'em? Good. Here we go:

1. Place your first cake layer on your cake plate (or board), making sure that it rests in the center of the plate.
2. Using your offset spatula, scoop about 1 cup of frosting onto the top of your cake layer.
3. Push and press the frosting around the cake layer, going all the way to the edges, using the bottom broad side of your offset spatula until the

layer is completely covered. Use the force of your forearm (not your wrist!) to push the frosting across the cake. No dainty spreading—you are the boss of the frosting, so push it around!

4. When you get your frosting level and smooth, center the other cake layer on top as precisely as possible.

5. Repeat steps 2 and 3 for the top of the second layer. Make sure that the frosting sticks out over the top edge of the entire cake.

6. Now we need to frost the sides with a crumb coat. The crumb coat seals in the crumbs and makes the final coat go on nice and smooth. Don't worry if this step doesn't look so pretty—the goal is to get all those crumbs sealed in so that the final coat is smooth and beautiful.

7. Scoop some frosting on the top of your offset spatula blade and press it into the side of your cake, holding the offset spatula perpendicular to the cake plate.

8. Without pulling the offset spatula from the side of the cake, push the frosting into the cake while rotating your cake plate in a single direction. (Don't backtrack, or you risk pulling the frosting off the cake and causing more crumbs.) Add more frosting as needed while you make your way around the entire cake until you get a thin layer of frosting on the cake. You can scrape the crumby frosting into your clean empty bowl before dipping back into your pretty frosting to avoid any crumby contamination.

9. As you frost, make sure you push the frosting all the way to the bottom edge of the cake as well as to the top edge to make sure all the cake is covered.

10. Scrape any excess frosting that is peeking up above the top edge of the cake across the top toward the center of the cake.

11. Remember, this step should not look finished. You just want to make sure that your edges are straight and that the crumbs are sealed inside the frosting.

12. Place the cake in the refrigerator to let the crumb coat set for about twenty minutes before applying your final coat.

13. To apply the final coat, remove the cake from the fridge and place it back on your turntable.

14. Your top should already be smooth and crumb-free, but if it isn't, place a scoop of frosting on top and push it back and forth until it reaches out over the top edge of the cake.

15. Now you can frost the sides just as you did for the crumb coat, adding a bit more frosting so that it is about 1/4 to 1/2 inch thick on the sides.

16. Push the frosting in and up as you go around the cake so that it creates a little excess of frosting peeking up over the top edge.

17. Pull that excess straight across the top toward the center, rotating the cake as you work your way around. The top should be flat and level.

18. If you'd like to put a textured look on the cake, use a cake comb or a serrated bread knife. Hold the cake comb or knife edge flat against the sides of your cake as you rotate the turntable. This will give a nice, even texture to the sides. Gently, please, you just want to add texture. Don't scrape all of the frosting off the dang thing! If you don't have a cake comb or prefer a smooth look, here's a trick. Fill a glass with hot water. Place the clean blade of your offset spatula in the water for five seconds and shake off any excess water. Hold the warm blade vertically against the side of your cake and rotate your cake. Voilà! Smooth edges!

19. Finish the bottom edge with the frosting border of your choice (keep reading, the instructions are below).

Hold on a sec, there. "What about my beautiful lemon curd?" you ask. "How do I get that lovely filling into my cake?"

FILLINGS

1. Frost your cake using steps 1 through 3 above.
2. Now get your frosting bag, fitted with a star tip, and fill it half full with your frosting. Pipe a ring around the top of your frosted cake layer so that it makes a 1/2-inch wall or dam to prevent your filling from seeping out to the edge.
3. Scoop 1/2 to 3/4 cup of your filling inside the dam and use a small offset spatula to spread the filling evenly across the cake layer, making sure not to go higher than your piped frosting dam. Now you can follow the rest of the frosting steps above to finish your cake!

Note: If you are using ganache as a filling, refrigerate the single cake layer for twenty minutes to allow the ganache to set completely before topping it with your second layer. If you skip this step, your top layer will slide back and forth when you try to frost the cake, and your dam will break, causing major ganache leakage!

FINISHING TOUCHES

Here are a few things you can try to make your gorgeous frosted cake a true masterpiece.

BORDERS   If you like, you can create a border of frosting around your cake. Some cakes get a top and bottom border, some just get one on the bottom, and others just get the top. You get to decide when and where to add the border.

Borders take some practice, and there are many tips to choose from. The star makes a fluffy shell border that is very traditional, while a round tip can make a simple beaded border that is more elegant and a bit more delicate. These techniques can't be taught by reading instructions; you really need a visual. So go to our YouTube channel, stickyfingersdc, and check out some of our tutorials! We'll teach you a traditional shell border, a reverse shell (great for the tops of cakes), and a beaded border.

CRUNCH   So you have your nice smooth cake frosted in a delicious almond crème frosting. You want to add some crunch and flavor with [insert desired crunchy bit here], but where do you put them? Around the outside of your cake, of course!

1. Hold your cake in one hand and position it over your tray of toasted nuts.
2. Take a handful of crunchies in your other hand and press them into the side of your cake, making sure the excess nuts fall back onto your tray so as not to waste.
3. Continue this until you have covered the cake sides all the way around.

For cakes covered in nuts, you can add your border to the top edge of your cake, since there are nuts at the bottom. This procedure works great with any nuts, including shredded coconut. Go get nutty! It also works great with chocolate chips, chocolate shavings, sprinkles, or crushed cookies (gingersnaps on the outside of Spice Cake, anyone?). Be creative, and let your taste buds guide you!

FRUIT   Adding fruit to your cake is a fantastic way to add color and flavor at the same time. Pipe some nice big dollops around the top edge of your cake to create pedestals for strawberries, or create a mound of raspberries in the center of your cake. You can even use blueberries as a border. You can't go wrong. Just be careful when putting sliced fruit on the outside of your cake. Those juices are going to start to break down your frosting pretty quickly (not to mention that the fruit itself will start to wilt), so it's best to add sliced fruit just before you are ready to serve the cake.

For Chocolate Lovers

The following recipes are all under the chocolate section because they all use the same techniques and basic ingredients, and utilize the magic of the baking soda-acid combo.

Make sure you are all set to go with this one. Grease pans or fill cupcake tins with liners; get your bowls and utensils on standby, and have your ingredients at the ready.

Each ingredient has a job and must work with the others to create a fluffy, soft, beautiful cake. You are basically relying on the reaction of the vinegar, baking soda, cocoa powder, and coffee to get those all-important bubbles we spoke of earlier. Baking soda reacts with the acid in the coffee and vinegar to give us the coveted power of CO_2, while the flavor from the coffee and the cocoa powder disguise the flavor of the baking soda. Vinegar is the strongest player on the team and causes the fastest reaction, which is why we save it for the very last step. Using a higher-fat cocoa powder will help keep your crumb from crumbling but will still get the job done with the baking soda.

If we want a fluffy, spongy cake, then we need to get it in the oven before the CO_2 bubbles stop bubbling. Those extra steam bubbles will be the icing on the cake once they are encapsulated, as the protein and starch cook to form the cells around those gasses. The oil coats those cells, giving us a moist and smooth mouthfeel.

Note: You have only a few precious seconds once the vinegar is mixed into the batter before your reaction begins, and your batter needs heat to trap those bubbles, so work fast. All you are looking for once the vinegar goes in is a slight color change swirling in the batter. Stop once you see color change and swirling—don't try to get it completely one color. By then it will be too late.

Ready, set, go!

Chocolate Love Cake

Start with chocolate baby steps to reach your dreams of chocolate abundance and overload with Chocolate Love.

Makes one 9-inch round two-layer cake or 18 cupcakes

1 ¾ cups plus 1 ½ tablespoons (9.2 ounces) all-purpose flour

1 ¼ cups plus 3 tablespoons (10 ounces) sugar

¾ cup (3 ounces) cocoa powder

2 teaspoons baking soda

½ teaspoon salt

1 ¼ cups water

⅓ cup vegetable or canola oil

½ cup brewed coffee, cooled

1 teaspoon vanilla extract

1 tablespoon vinegar (recommended: apple cider vinegar)

Chocolate Frosting (recipe follows)

1. Preheat the oven to 350°F.
2. Line two 9-inch round cake pans with parchment paper, or lightly oil and dust with flour.
3. Whisk the flour, sugar, cocoa powder, baking soda, and salt into a medium bowl. Set the bowl aside.
4. In a small bowl, whisk together the water, oil, coffee, and vanilla.
5. Add the wet ingredients to the dry ingredients and whisk until just incorporated.
6. Fold in the vinegar until you begin to see streaks. See Note on page 28 for reference. Do not overmix the batter.
7. Distribute the batter evenly between the two pans. Bake for 20 to 25 minutes, until the cake springs back to the touch.
8. Place the pans on a cooling rack to cool completely, then run a knife or

plastic dough scraper around the edges of the pans to loosen the cakes from the sides. Turn the pans upside down to remove the cakes.

9. If you are making cupcakes, fill 18 lined cupcake cups three-quarters full and bake for 16 to 19 minutes, until a toothpick inserted in the center comes out clean. Place the cupcake tins on a cooling rack to cool completely, then turn the tins upside down to remove the cupcakes.

10. Frost with the chocolate frosting (see pages 22–25 for prepping and frosting techniques).

Chocolate Frosting

Makes enough to frost one 9-inch round two-layer cake or 18 cupcakes

1 cup plus 2 tablespoons non-hydrogenated vegetable shortening (recommended: Earth Balance)

¼ cup plus 2 tablespoons non-hydrogenated vegan margarine (recommended: Earth Balance)

3 ¾ cups (1 pound, 1 ounce) powdered sugar

¾ cup (3 ounces) cocoa powder

1 ½ teaspoons vanilla extract

3 to 5 tablespoons soymilk, as needed

1. In the bowl of a stand mixer, combine the shortening and margarine and whip with the paddle attachment until completely combined. Scrape the bottom of the bowl to ensure that the ingredients are mixed thoroughly.

2. On low speed, slowly add the powdered sugar and cocoa powder a little at a time.

3. Once the powdered sugar and cocoa powder are incorporated, add the vanilla and soymilk and mix on low speed until the liquids are incorporated and the desired consistency is reached.

4. Scrape the bottom of the bowl and mix on medium-high speed until all the ingredients are combined and the frosting is fluffy, about 2 minutes.

Love Bite

Cocoa Powder

Move over, green tea. The news we've all been waiting for . . . cocoa powder is good for you!

Cup for cup, cocoa powder has three times more antioxidants than brewed green tea. The chemicals responsible for giving the bean its color are also responsible for helping fight what ails you, oh, like heart disease and cancer. And (news flash) it's been reported to boost your mood and give you a sense of well-being. Okay, so we're not going to start downing mass quantities of the stuff, since it is best combined with sugar and fat (mmmm, frosting). But you'll be glad to know that you get a double whammy of goodness with vegan cocoa-rich recipes. No cholesterol, healthier sugars, less saturated fats, and antioxidants in your cake? What's better than that?

Chocolate Mocha Cake

The frosting on this cake will be habit forming, as are the flavors that make it so good. Don't be alarmed if you go through withdrawal when it's gone.

Makes one 9-inch round two-layer cake or 18 cupcakes

Chocolate Love Cake (page 29)
Mocha Frosting (recipe follows)

1. Make the cake according to the instructions on pages 29–30 and frost with the mocha frosting. See pages 22–25 for prepping and frosting techniques.

Mocha Frosting

Makes enough to frost one 9-inch two-layer cake or 18 cupcakes

1 cup plus 2 tablespoons non-hydrogenated vegetable shortening (recommended: Earth Balance)

¼ cup plus 2 tablespoons non-hydrogenated vegan margarine (recommended: Earth Balance)

3 ¾ cups (1 pound, 1 ounce) powdered sugar

¾ cup (3 ounces) cocoa powder

3 tablespoons brewed espresso, cooled

2 to 3 tablespoons soymilk

1. In the bowl of a stand mixer, combine the shortening and margarine and whip with the paddle attachment until completely combined. Scrape the bottom of the bowl to ensure that the ingredients are mixed thoroughly.
2. On low speed, slowly add the powdered sugar and cocoa powder a little at a time.

3. Once the powdered sugar and cocoa powder are incorporated, add the espresso and soymilk and mix on low speed until the liquids are incorporated and the desired consistency is reached.
4. Scrape the bottom of the bowl and mix on medium-high speed until all the ingredients are combined and the frosting is fluffy, about 2 minutes.

Love Bite

Coffee

The more you drink, the less likely you are to develop type 2 diabetes. Studies show that drinking more than six cups of coffee a day reduces the risk, and the benefits increase with every cup you drink. According to Frank Hu, M.D., MPH, Ph.D., nutrition and epidemiology professor at the Harvard School of Public Health, it's the whole package: The benefits come from an array of antioxidants and minerals that are found in both caffeinated and decaf coffee. And scientists here at Sticky Fingers are working tirelessly to prove the beneficial effects. Hard at work in our tasty laboratory, we've discovered more than one way for you to get your daily dose of joe!

Cookies-n-Cake

Our take on cookies and crème flavored favorites—minus the milk, of course! This is our best seller, next to chocolate cake, and is a great addition to any dessert table. Go crazy and think outside the cookie box! We use Newman-O's for our crumb, but any crunchy variety will do!

Makes one 9-inch round two-layer cake or 18 cupcakes

Chocolate Love Cake (page 29)
Cookie Frosting (recipe follows)

1. Make the cake according to the instructions on pages 29–30 and frost with the cookie frosting (see pages 22–25 for prepping and frosting techniques).

Cookie Frosting

Makes enough to frost one 9-inch round two-layer cake or 18 cupcakes

1 cup plus 2 tablespoons non-hydrogenated vegetable shortening (recommended: Earth Balance)

¼ cup plus 2 tablespoons non-hydrogenated vegan margarine (recommended: Earth Balance)

4 ½ cups (1 pound, 4 ounces) powdered sugar

3 ½ teaspoons vanilla extract

2 to 4 tablespoons soymilk, as needed

½ cup favorite cookie crumbs (optional; see Note)

1. In the bowl of a stand mixer, combine the shortening and margarine and whip with the paddle attachment until completely combined. Scrape the bottom of the bowl to ensure that the ingredients are mixed thoroughly.

2. On low speed, slowly add the powdered sugar a little at a time.

3. Once the sugar is incorporated, add the vanilla and then the soymilk, 1 tablespoon at a time, and mix on low speed until the liquids are incorporated and the desired consistency is reached.

4. Scrape the bottom of the bowl and mix on medium-high speed until all the ingredients are combined and the frosting is fluffy, about 2 minutes.

5. If using, stir cookie crumbs into the frosting until they are evenly incorporated.

NOTE

A few pulses in your trusty food processor work like a charm for turning your cookies into bits. No food processor? Use a plastic bag: Fill it with your crunchy favorite, and put that rolling pin to work. Stir in your newly crushed cookies.

Peanut Butter Fudge Cake

It's been said before, and we'll say it again—two great tastes that go great together! There's just no messing with perfection!

Makes one 9-inch round two-layer cake or 18 cupcakes

Chocolate Love Cake (page 29)
Peanut Butter Frosting (recipe follows)
½ cup crushed peanuts for sprinkling (optional)
¼ cup melted, cooled chocolate for drizzling (optional)

1. Make the cake according to the instructions on pages 29–30 and frost with the peanut butter frosting (see pages 22–25 for prepping and frosting techniques).
2. Added bonus: Sprinkle with crushed peanuts and drizzle with melted chocolate for an extra peanut-chocolate explosion!

Peanut Butter Frosting

Makes enough to frost one 9-inch round two-layer cake or 18 cupcakes

2 ½ cups plus 2 tablespoons smooth peanut butter (recommended: Skippy Natural)
1 cup non-hydrogenated vegetable shortening (recommended: Earth Balance)
1 cup non-hydrogenated vegan margarine (recommended: Earth Balance)
6 cups (1 pound, 11 ounces) powdered sugar
½ to ¾ cup soymilk

1. In the bowl of a stand mixer, combine the peanut butter, shortening, and margarine and whip with the paddle attachment until light and fluffy, 5 to 7

minutes. Scrape the bottom of the bowl to ensure that the ingredients are mixed thoroughly.

2. On low speed, slowly add the powdered sugar a little at a time.

3. Once the sugar is incorporated, add the soymilk and mix on low until the liquid is incorporated and the desired consistency is reached.

4. Scrape the bottom of the bowl and mix on medium-high speed until all the ingredients are combined and frosting is fluffy, about 2 minutes.

Choco Raspberry Dream

My love affair with the raspberry began the first time I ever went raspberry picking. Greig Farm in Red Hook, New York, was right down the road from our house. We went there every chance we got, or at least when my parents gave in to my begging and pleading. Back to the story. I forced through the swarming bees (which also love raspberries) and popped one right into my mouth, filled with the warmth of the summer sun. They should have weighed me before and after, because there were way more berries in my belly than in my basket.

We've created a berry-great flavor cluster by teaming up with double chocolate! So rich and delicious, a fabulous and farm-friendly pairing!

Makes one 9-inch round two-layer cake or 18 cupcakes

2 cups (10 ounces) all-purpose flour

1 ¼ cups plus 3 tablespoons (10 ounces) sugar

¾ cup (3 ounces) cocoa powder

2 teaspoons baking soda

½ teaspoon salt

1 ¼ cups coconut milk (recommended: So Delicious)

⅓ cup vegetable or canola oil

½ cup brewed coffee, cooled

4 ounces good-quality dark chocolate, melted

1 teaspoon vanilla extract

2 teaspoons vinegar (recommended: apple cider vinegar)

Raspberry Frosting (recipe follows)

Chocolate Ganache (recipe follows)

1 cup fresh raspberries for topping

1. Preheat the oven to 350°F.
2. Line two 9-inch round cake pans with parchment paper, or lightly oil and dust with flour.
3. Whisk the flour, sugar, cocoa powder, baking soda, and salt into a medium bowl. Set the bowl aside.

4. In a small bowl, whisk together the coconut milk, oil, coffee, melted chocolate, and vanilla.

5. Add the wet ingredients to the dry ingredients and whisk until just incorporated.

6. Fold in the vinegar until you begin to see streaks. See Note on page 28 for reference. Do not overmix the batter.

7. Distribute the batter evenly between the 2 pans.

8. Bake for 20 minutes, or until the cakes spring back to the touch.

9. Place the pans on a cooling rack to cool completely, then run a knife or plastic dough scraper around the edges of the pan to loosen the cake from the sides. Turn the pans upside down onto the rack to remove the cakes.

10. If you are making cupcakes, fill 18 lined cupcake cups three-quarters full and bake for 16 to 19 minutes, until a toothpick inserted in the center comes out clean. Place the cupcake tins on a cooling rack to cool completely, then turn the tins upside down to remove the cupcakes.

11. Frost your cake with the raspberry frosting (see pages 22–25 for prepping and frosting techniques).

12. Make sure your ganache is pourable but not hot to the touch, as you don't want to melt your frosting. With a spoon or a glass measuring pitcher, pour the ganache in the center of the cake until it reaches the sides. Pour a small amount along the edge, enough so you get a few drips running over the sides. Let the ganache set before moving the cake around or you risk losing your frosting and your ganache in a topping avalanche. Top with fresh raspberries.

13. If you are making cupcakes, frost them however you like, with a round or star tip, or even by hand. You want those ridges! Then fill a piping bag one-quarter full with ganache, cut a small part of the tip off, and drizzle the ganache over the cupcake. More chocolate is what you desire? Then dip the entire top of the frosted cupcake into the ganache. Chocolate-covered raspberry heaven.

Raspberry Frosting

Makes enough to frost one 9-inch round two-layer cake or 18 cupcakes

1 cup plus 2 tablespoons non-hydrogenated vegetable shortening (recommended: Earth Balance)

¼ cup plus 2 tablespoons non-hydrogenated vegan margarine (recommended: Earth Balance)

⅓ cup raspberry puree (store-bought or homemade; see Note)

4 ¼ cups (1 pound, 3 ounces) powdered sugar

1 ½ tablespoons lemon juice

1. In the bowl of a stand mixer, combine the shortening and margarine and whip with the paddle attachment until completely combined. Scrape the bottom of the bowl to ensure that the ingredients are mixed thoroughly.
2. Add the raspberry puree and mix until incorporated. Scrape the bottom of the bowl to ensure that the puree is mixed thoroughly.
3. On low speed, slowly add the powdered sugar a little at a time.
4. Add the lemon juice and mix to combine. Scrape the bottom of the bowl and mix on medium-high speed until all the ingredients are combined and the frosting is fluffy, about 2 minutes.

NOTE

To make homemade berry puree: Heat 1 ½ cups fresh or frozen berries in a medium heavy-bottomed saucepan over medium-high heat, stirring constantly until they break down, about 15 minutes. Remove from heat and blend with an electric hand blender, then return to the heat and cook down until most of the liquid is evaporated, about 15 minutes. Let cool completely before using.

Chocolate Ganache

Makes 1 cup

½ cup coconut creamer (recommended: So Delicious)
8 ounces 70% dark chocolate, chopped, or pistoles

1. Heat the coconut creamer in the top part of a double boiler over medium heat until steaming. Do not boil.
2. Place the chocolate in a heatproof bowl, pour the hot creamer over the chocolate, and let sit for 30 seconds.
3. Whisk the coconut creamer and chocolate until the chocolate is melted and the two ingredients are completely combined. The ganache should be thick but still pourable.

Ganache

Ganache isn't just for the inside of your cake. It looks wonderfully decadent when you pour it over your cake, too! There are a couple of ways to go about getting ganache atop your cake.

1. First up, after you frost your cake with a smooth layer of frosting, you can pour ganache over the entire cake to create a glorious chocolaty shine.
2. Just make sure you take your cake off the cake plate and place it on a cooling rack set over a sheet pan. That way, the excess ganache pours and gathers in your sheet pan rather than on your plate. And you can reuse any ganache drippings you catch.

3. Pour your ganache on top of the cake, letting it pool up in the center.

4. Use your offset spatula to spread the ganache toward the edges of the cake, working slowly toward each edge. The ganache will begin to spill down the sides to cover your cake.

5. Slowly add more ganache until the entire cake is covered.

6. Make sure the ganache on the top of your cake is not on too thick. You want a thin layer coating the entire cake.

7. Place the cake in the refrigerator (sheet pan and all) to firm up for 20 minutes.

8. Take your offset spatula and run it around and under the bottom edge of your cake to release any ganache that might be clinging to the cooling rack.

9. Using your offset spatula, lift the cake off the cooling rack and place it back onto your cake plate.

10. Add a bottom border if you wish.

You can also use the ganache to cover the top of your cake and create a drippy look down the sides. You can leave the cake on the cake plate for this one:

1. Pour about 1 cup of your ganache on top of your cake, letting it pool up in the center.

2. Use your offset spatula to spread the ganache toward the edges of the cake until it begins to drip down the sides.

3. Don't add too much ganache, because you don't want the entire cake to be covered. You just want the top covered with big chocolate drips clinging to the edges.

El Caliente:
Chocolate Spice Cake

Adding cayenne pepper to your chocolate cake can really give it a zing! But beware, cayenne varies in intensity, so test before you add. If it sets your mouth on fire, you may want to hold back a bit. We call the frosting in this cake recipe "Mexican" because the combo of spice and cocoa originated there, right in the middle of the ancient Aztec and Maya culture. The Spaniards stole, I mean, "discovered" the sacred ingredient, and it was quickly brought back to Europe for everyone to enjoy. So delicious in its pure form, even its name sounds so close to the original Mayan word, *cacahuatl*.

Makes one 9-inch round two-layer cake or 18 cupcakes

1 ¾ cups plus 1 ½ tablespoons (9.2 ounces) all-purpose flour

1 ¼ cups plus 3 tablespoons (10 ounces) sugar

⅔ cup (2.5 ounces) cocoa powder

2 teaspoons ground cinnamon

2 teaspoons baking soda

1 teaspoon cayenne pepper

½ teaspoon salt

1 ½ cups coconut milk (recommended: So Delicious)

⅔ cup canola or vegetable oil

½ cup brewed coffee, cooled

1 teaspoon vanilla extract

2 teaspoons vinegar (recommended: apple cider vinegar)

Mexican Chocolate Frosting (recipe follows)

1. Preheat the oven to 350°F.
2. Line two 9-inch round cake pans with parchment paper, or lightly oil and dust with flour.
3. Whisk the flour, sugar, cocoa powder, cinnamon, baking soda, cayenne pepper, and salt into a medium bowl. Set the bowl aside.
4. In a small bowl, whisk together the coconut milk, oil, coffee, and vanilla.

5. Add the wet ingredients to the dry ingredients and whisk until just incorporated.

6. Fold in the vinegar until you begin to see streaks. See Note on page 28 for reference. Do not overmix the batter.

7. Distribute the batter evenly between the two pans. Bake for 20 to 25 minutes, until the cakes spring back to the touch.

8. Place the pans on a cooling rack to cool completely, then run a knife or plastic dough scraper around the edges of the pans to loosen the cakes from the sides. Turn the pans upside down to remove the cakes.

9. If you are making cupcakes, fill 18 lined cupcake cups three-quarters full and bake for 16 to 19 minutes, until a toothpick inserted in the center comes out clean. Place the cupcake tins on a cooling rack to cool completely, then turn the tins upside down to remove the cupcakes.

10. Frost with the Mexican chocolate frosting (see pages 22–25 for prepping and frosting techniques).

Mexican Chocolate Frosting

Makes enough to frost one 9-inch round two-layer cake or 18 cupcakes

1 cup plus 2 tablespoons non-hydrogenated vegetable shortening (recommended: Earth Balance)

¼ cup plus 2 tablespoons non-hydrogenated vegan margarine (recommended: Earth Balance)

3 ¾ cups (1 pound, 1 ounce) powdered sugar

¾ cup (3 ounces) cocoa powder

1 to 2 teaspoons cayenne pepper, to taste

1 ½ teaspoons ground cinnamon

1 ½ teaspoons vanilla extract

3 to 5 tablespoons soymilk, as needed

1. In the bowl of a stand mixer, combine the shortening and margarine and whip with the paddle attachment until completely combined. Scrape the bottom of the bowl to ensure that the ingredients are mixed thoroughly.

2. Whisk the powdered sugar, cocoa powder, cayenne pepper, and cinnamon into a medium bowl.

3. On low speed, slowly add the powdered sugar mixture to the shortening mixture a little at a time.

4. Once the powdered sugar mixture is incorporated, add the vanilla and soymilk and mix on low until the liquids are incorporated and the desired consistency is reached.

5. Scrape the bottom of the bowl and mix on medium-high speed until all the ingredients are combined and the frosting is fluffy, about 2 minutes.

Love Bite

Cayenne

Cayenne, the red-headed wonder of the pepper world. Most folks are afraid of spice, eschewing that picante and cowering from the caliente. But those red locks hold more than just good looks and hot flavor! That spicy kick isn't just making you sweat, it's also raising your metabolism while you eat and digest. Digesting is its other talent, helping your tummy stay healthy; it has even been known to help cure ulcers. Who would have guessed that this hot little number could be this talented? But the most insane fact about cayenne is how perfectly it pairs with chocolate.

Red Velvet Cake

Velvet is a given if you follow this recipe to a T, but red is another story. Red intensity depends on the strength of your food color. We like to use as little as possible because no one likes red tongues. Natural coloring is a great choice as well, but the colors will not be as bright as the unnatural stuff. The type of cocoa powder you use can affect the color, too. Red cocoa powder (Dutched, 24% cocoa butter) is all the rage right now. Try it!

The cream cheese icing is my husband, Peter's, favorite frosting. Every year for his birthday he asks for the frosting before the cake flavor. He'll take it with any cake: red velvet cake, chocolate whiskey cake, coconut cake, or strawberry cake. These may not all sound like good combinations, but in fact they are are heavenly. My husband is a cream cheese frosting connoisseur.

Makes one 9-inch round two-layer cake or 18 cupcakes

2 cups plus 3 tablespoons (11 ounces) all-purpose flour

1 cup plus 3 tablespoons (8.5 ounces) sugar

1 tablespoon cocoa powder

2 teaspoons baking soda

¼ teaspoon salt

2/3 cup water

¼ cup plus 1 tablespoon soymilk

¼ cup plus 1 tablespoon coconut milk (recommended: So Delicious)

¼ cup canola or vegetable oil

½ tablespoon lemon juice

1 teaspoon vanilla extract

1 teaspoon liquid red food coloring

2 teaspoons vinegar (recommended: apple cider vinegar)

Cream Cheese Frosting (recipe follows)

1. Preheat the oven to 350°F.

2. Line two 9-inch round cake pans with parchment paper, or lightly oil and dust with flour.

3. Whisk the flour, sugar, cocoa powder, baking soda, and salt into a medium bowl. Set the bowl aside.

4. In a small bowl, whisk together the water, soymilk, coconut milk, oil, lemon juice, vanilla, and red food coloring.

5. Add the wet ingredients to the dry ingredients and whisk until just incorporated.

6. Fold in the vinegar until you begin to see streaks. See Note on page 28 for reference. Do not overmix the batter.

7. Distribute the batter evenly between the two pans. Bake for 20 to 25 minutes, until the cakes spring back to the touch.

8. Place the pans on a cooling rack to cool completely, then run a knife or plastic dough scraper around the edges of the pans to loosen the cakes from the sides. Turn the pans upside down to remove the cakes.

9. If you are making cupcakes, fill 18 lined cupcake cups three-quarters full and bake for 16 to 19 minutes, until a toothpick inserted in the center comes out clean. Place the cupcake tins on a cooling rack to cool completely, then turn the pans upside down to remove the cupcakes.

10. Frost with the cream cheese frosting (see pages 22–25 for prepping and frosting techniques).

Cream Cheese Frosting

Makes enough to frost one 9-inch round two-layer cake or 18 cupcakes

1 cup non-hydrogenated vegetable shortening (recommended: Earth Balance)

12 ounces non-hydrogenated vegan cream cheese (recommended: Tofutti), softened

4 1/2 cups (1 pound, 4 ounces) powdered sugar

1 tablespoon vanilla extract

1 1/2 teaspoons lemon juice

2 to 4 drops lemon oil, to taste

1. In the bowl of an electric mixer fitted with the paddle attachment, beat the shortening until smooth.
2. Add the cream cheese and beat until well combined.
3. Add the powdered sugar, vanilla, lemon juice, and lemon oil and beat just until smooth. (The frosting can be made in advance, covered, and refrigerated; let stand at room temperature to soften before using.)

Classic Vanilla Cake

Classic style is always in demand. No exceptions here! Learn this recipe for basic vanilla and you will be well on your way to making the classiest cakes around.

Makes one 9-inch round two-layer cake or 18 cupcakes

2 ¼ cups plus 1 tablespoon (11.5 ounces) all-purpose flour

1 tablespoon baking powder

½ teaspoon salt

1 ¼ cups (8.8 ounces) sugar

½ cup non-hydrogenated vegan margarine (recommended: Earth Balance)

1 ½ teaspoons egg replacer (recommended: Ener-G)

½ cup water

¾ cup soymilk

2 teaspoons vanilla extract

Vanilla Frosting (recipe follows)

1. Preheat the oven to 350°F.
2. Line two 9-inch round cake pans with parchment paper, or lightly oil and dust with flour.
3. Whisk the flour, baking powder, and salt into a medium bowl. Set the bowl aside.
4. In the bowl of an electric stand mixer, combine the sugar and margarine, and cream with the whisk attachment, about 5 minutes. Scrape down the sides and bottom of the bowl to ensure that the ingredients are incorporated.
5. In a small bowl or cup, combine the egg replacer and water and stir to dissolve the egg replacer. Add the egg replacer to the sugar mixture and mix until combined.

6. In a small bowl, combine the soymilk and vanilla and set aside.

7. Turn the mixer speed to low and slowly add the dry ingredients and the soymilk mixture, alternating between the two and ending with the soymilk.

8. Distribute the batter evenly between the two pans. Bake for 18 to 25 minutes, until a toothpick inserted in the middle comes out clean or the cakes spring back to the touch.

9. Place the pans on a cooling rack to cool completely, then run a knife or plastic dough scraper around the edges of the pans to loosen the cakes from the sides. Turn the pans upside down to remove the cakes.

10. If you are making cupcakes, fill 18 lined cupcake cups three-quarters full and bake for 16 to 19 minutes, until a toothpick inserted in the center comes out clean. Place the cupcake tins on a cooling rack to cool completely, then turn the pans upside down to remove the cupcakes.

11. Frost with the vanilla frosting (see pages 22–25 for prepping and frosting techniques).

Vanilla Frosting

Makes enough to frost one 9-inch round two-layer cake or 18 cupcakes

1 cup plus 2 tablespoons non-hydrogenated vegetable shortening (recommended: Earth Balance)

¼ cup plus 2 tablespoons non-hydrogenated vegan margarine (recommended: Earth Balance)

4 ½ cups (1 pound, 4 ounces) powdered sugar

3 ½ teaspoons vanilla extract

2 to 4 tablespoons soymilk, as needed

1. In the bowl of a stand mixer, combine the shortening and margarine and whip with the paddle attachment until completely combined. Scrape the bottom of the bowl to ensure that the ingredients are mixed thoroughly.
2. On low speed, slowly add the powdered sugar a little at a time.
3. Once the powdered sugar is incorporated, on low speed, add the vanilla, then the soymilk, 1 tablespoon at a time, and mix until the liquids are incorporated and the desired consistency is reached.
4. Scrape the bottom of the bowl and mix on medium-high speed until all the ingredients are combined and the frosting is fluffy, about 2 minutes.

Tiramisu

For our tiramisu cake and cupcakes, we brush our vanilla cake with lots of espresso, layer or fill with tiramisu filling, complement with coffee frosting, and dust with cocoa powder to enhance its good looks, making it as stunning on the outside as it is within. Tiramisu is all about proper layering to obtain the best vanilla cake, coffee flavor, and filling ratios. Here's how.

Makes one 9-inch round two-layer cake or 18 cupcakes

Classic Vanilla Cake (page 49)
½ cup espresso or strong brewed
   coffee, cooled
Coffee Frosting (recipe follows)

Tiramisu Filling (recipe
   follows)
Cocoa powder for dusting
Coffee beans for topping

1. Using a pastry brush, brush the entire top of one cooled vanilla cake layer with espresso until coated.
2. Using a pastry bag with a large round tip (or cut a ½-inch-diameter hole in the bag), pipe a complete ring of coffee frosting around the edge of the cake, about ¼ inch in from the side. This is to hold in the filling.
3. Spoon and spread about ½ cup of tiramisu filling evenly over the bottom layer. Top with the second cake layer and repeat, brushing with espresso, piping a ring of coffee frosting around the edge, and spreading ½ cup of tiramisu filling over the top.
4. Sprinkle with cocoa powder, top with a coffee bean, and serve.
5. If you are making cupcakes, once they have cooled, cut or spoon out about ½ inch from the top of a cupcake. With a pastry brush, brush the top of the cupcake and the center of the hole with espresso.
6. Using a pastry bag with a large round tip (or cut a ½-inch-diameter hole in the bag), pipe a complete ring of coffee frosting around the edge of your

cupcake. Fill the center with as much tiramisu filling as possible, either with a spoon or a piping bag.

7. Sprinkle with cocoa powder and top with a coffee bean. Repeat with the remaining cupcakes.

Coffee Frosting

Makes enough to frost one 9-inch round two-layer cake or 18 cupcakes

1 cup plus 2 tablespoons non-hydrogenated vegetable shortening (recommended: Earth Balance)

¼ cup plus 2 tablespoons non-hydrogenated vegan margarine (recommended: Earth Balance)

4 ½ cups (1 pound, 4 ounces) powdered sugar

3 tablespoons brewed espresso, cooled

2 to 4 tablespoons soymilk, as needed

1. In the bowl of a stand mixer, combine the shortening and margarine and whip with the paddle attachment until completely combined. Scrape the bottom of the bowl to ensure that the ingredients are mixed thoroughly.

2. On low speed, slowly add the powdered sugar a little at a time.

3. Once the powdered sugar is incorporated, add the espresso and soymilk and mix on low speed until the liquids are incorporated and the desired consistency is reached.

4. Scrape the bottom of the bowl and mix on medium-high speed until all the ingredients are combined and the frosting is fluffy, about 2 minutes.

Tiramisu Filling

Makes enough to frost one 9-inch round layer cake or 18 cupcakes

1 cup soymilk

4 tablespoons (1.6 ounces) sugar

2 tablespoons rum

1 tablespoon egg replacer
(recommended: Ener-G)

2 tablespoons silken tofu

2 tablespoons cornstarch

8 ounces non-hydrogenated vegan
cream cheese (recommended:
Tofutti), softened

1. In a medium, heavy-bottomed saucepan, heat the soymilk with 2 tablespoons of the sugar over medium heat and stir until the sugar dissolves. Do not boil.

2. In a blender or food processor, combine the rum, egg replacer, tofu, cornstarch, and the remaining 2 tablespoons sugar and puree until smooth.

3. Add the tofu mixture to the saucepan with the hot soymilk. Continue to cook, stirring, until the mixture becomes very thick, about 5 minutes.

4. Pour the hot mixture into a container and let rest at room temperature until cooled. Cover and refrigerate for at least 2 hours.

5. Add the cream cheese and blend with an electric hand blender until smooth. Cover and refrigerate until ready to use.

6. For a creamier and lighter texture, whip in the cream cheese right before you add the mixture to your dessert.

7. Extra filling can be stored in an airtight container and refrigerated for up to 1 week.

Love Bite

....

The Thermic Effect of Food

The mere act of digesting food requires calories and accounts for nearly 10 percent of your calorie burn. What could be more mind-blowing than that? Well, spicy foods enhance the effect by prolonging the burn, not just in your mouth but all throughout that hot bod of yours—by three hours! More? Can there be more? Caffeine has been shown to increase this effect up to 11 percent if ingested every two hours over a twelve-hour period. Well, don't just stand there looking astonished, grab a cup of coffee (or a dollop of coffee frosting) and start eating!

Boston Crème Cake

The pastry crème makes this cake. More, please! You will be making excuses to eat this classic cake creation every chance you get.

Makes one 9-inch round two-layer cake or 18 cupcakes

Classic Vanilla Cake (page 49)
Pastry Crème (recipe follows)
Chocolate Ganache (page 41)

1. Place one of the cooled cake layers flat side up (most likely bottom side up). Spoon the pastry crème over the cake, spreading to make an even layer.
2. Place the second cake layer (top side up) over the first layer.
3. Pour or spoon the ganache onto the center of the cake. Using an offset spatula, spread the ganache to the edges of the cake, allowing it to drip down the sides. Let the ganache set before serving.
4. If you are making cupcakes, cool them, and using a spoon or knife, cut out about ½ inch from the center of a cupcake. Carefully fill with pastry crème without cracking the cupcake.
5. Dip the top of the cupcake into the ganache. Repeat with the remaining cupcakes. Let set before serving.

Pastry Crème

Makes 1 ½ cups

1 cup soymilk	2 tablespoons silken tofu
4 tablespoons (1.6 ounces) sugar	2 tablespoons cornstarch
2 tablespoons water	2 teaspoons non-hydrogenated vegan margarine (recommended: Earth Balance)
1 tablespoon egg replacer (recommended: Ener-G)	1 teaspoon vanilla extract

1. In a medium heavy-bottomed saucepan, heat the soymilk with 2 tablespoons of the sugar over medium heat and stir until the sugar dissolves. Do not boil.

2. In a blender or food processor, combine the water, egg replacer, tofu, cornstarch, and the remaining 2 tablespoons sugar and puree until smooth.

3. Add the tofu mixture to the saucepan with the hot soymilk and cook, whisking continuously, until the mixture becomes very thick, about 5 minutes.

4. Remove from the heat and stir in the margarine and vanilla until melted and combined.

5. Pour the hot mixture into a container and let rest at room temperature until cooled. Cover and chill for at least 2 hours before using.

6. For a creamier and lighter texture, whip the pastry crème after it is firm and has set, just before you add it to your dessert.

Spice Cake

This is one of our newest additions to Sticky Fingers. After being on *Cupcake Wars*, we were inspired to start experimenting, and when we got home we went right for the spice cabinet.

Makes one 9-inch round two-layer cake or 18 cupcakes

2 tablespoons molasses

1/2 cup plus 1 1/2 tablespoons (4.2 ounces) sugar

1/2 cup plus 1/2 tablespoon (3.75 ounces) brown sugar

1 cup soymilk

1/2 cup plus 2 tablespoons canola or vegetable oil

1 teaspoon vanilla extract

2 1/2 cups plus 1 tablespoon (12.8 ounces) all-purpose flour

1 teaspoon baking powder

1/2 teaspoon baking soda

1/4 teaspoon salt

1 teaspoon ground cinnamon

1/4 teaspoon ground allspice

1/4 teaspoon ground ginger

1/4 teaspoon ground nutmeg

1/8 teaspoon ground cloves

Vanilla Hazelnut Frosting (recipe follows)

1 cup hazelnuts, toasted and crushed (see Note)

1. Preheat the oven to 350°F.
2. Line two 9-inch round cake pans with parchment paper, or lightly oil and dust with flour.
3. In the bowl of a stand mixer, combine the molasses, sugars, soymilk, oil, and vanilla, and cream with the paddle attachment until light and fluffy, 2 to 3 minutes. Scrape the bottom of the bowl to ensure that all the ingredients are incorporated.
4. In a separate bowl, whisk together the flour, baking powder, baking soda, salt, cinnamon, allspice, ginger, nutmeg, and cloves. Add to the sugar mixture and mix until just incorporated. Do not overmix the batter.

5. Distribute the batter evenly between the two pans. Bake for 15 to 20 minutes, until the cakes spring back to the touch.

6. Place the pans on a cooling rack to cool completely, then run a knife or plastic dough scraper around the edges of the pans to loosen the cakes from the sides. Turn the pans upside down to remove the cakes.

7. If you are making cupcakes, fill 18 lined cupcake cups three-quarters full and bake for 16 to 19 minutes, until a toothpick inserted in the center comes out clean. Place the cupcake tin on a cooling rack to cool completely, then turn the tin upside down to remove the cupcakes.

8. Frost with the vanilla hazelnut frosting (see pages 22–25 for prepping and frosting techniques) and top with toasted hazelnuts.

NOTE

To toast hazelnuts, preheat the oven to 350°F. Place the hazelnuts on a light-colored tray. Toast until lightly golden, 5 to 7 minutes. Be sure not to overbake the hazelnuts, as they will become too bitter to enjoy. You can pop the hazelnuts in the oven right after your cakes come out to make the most efficient use of the heat. Once cooled, crush the hazelnuts with the flat side of a knife or pulse for 10 seconds in a food processor.

Vanilla Hazelnut Frosting

Makes enough to frost one 9-inch round two-layer cake or 18 cupcakes

1 cup plus 2 tablespoons non-hydrogenated vegetable shortening (recommended: Earth Balance)

¼ cup plus 2 tablespoons non-hydrogenated vegan margarine (recommended: Earth Balance)

4 ½ cups (1 pound, 4 ounces) powdered sugar

3 ½ teaspoons vanilla extract

2 teaspoons hazelnut extract

2 to 4 tablespoons soymilk, as needed

1. In the bowl of a stand mixer, combine the shortening and margarine and whip with the paddle attachment until completely combined. Scrape the bottom of the bowl to ensure that the ingredients are mixed thoroughly.
2. On low speed, slowly add the powdered sugar a little at a time.
3. Once the sugar is incorporated, on low speed, add the vanilla and hazelnut extracts, then add the soymilk, 1 tablespoon at a time, and mix until the liquids are incorporated and the desired consistency is reached.
4. Scrape the bottom of the bowl and mix on medium-high speed until all the ingredients are combined and the frosting is fluffy, about 2 minutes.

Almond Crème Cake

L ight and delicious, pure decadence at its finest. It's not hard to believe that this is the number one wedding cake in our store. Try it and find out why.

Makes one 9-inch round two-layer cake or 18 cupcakes

Classic Vanilla Cake (page 49)
Vanilla Almond Frosting (recipe follows)
1 cup toasted sliced almonds for topping (optional; see Note)

1. Make the cake according to the instructions on pages 49–50 and frost with the vanilla almond frosting (see pages 22–25 for prepping and frosting techniques).
2. Added bonus: Press the toasted sliced almonds onto the side of your cake or atop your cupcakes.

NOTE

To toast almonds, preheat the oven to 350°F. Spread a layer of slivered or sliced almonds on a light-colored sheet pan and bake for 5 to 7 minutes, until golden. You can pop the almonds in the oven right after you take your cakes or cupcakes out to make efficient use of the heat. Be sure not to overbake your almonds— medium to dark brown means bitter.

Vanilla Almond Frosting

Makes enough to frost one 9-inch round two-layer cake or 18 cupcakes

1 cup plus 2 tablespoons non-hydrogenated vegetable shortening (recommended: Earth Balance)

¼ cup plus 2 tablespoons non-hydrogenated vegan margarine (recommended: Earth Balance)

4 ½ cups (1 pound, 4 ounces) powdered sugar

3 ½ teaspoons vanilla extract

2 teaspoons almond extract

2 to 4 tablespoons soymilk, as needed

1. In the bowl of a stand mixer, combine the shortening and margarine and whip with the paddle attachment until completely combined. Scrape the bottom of the bowl to ensure that the ingredients are mixed thoroughly.
2. On low speed, slowly add the powdered sugar a little at a time.
3. Once the powdered sugar is incorporated, on low speed, add the vanilla and almond extracts, then the soymilk, 1 tablespoon at a time, and mix until the liquids are incorporated and the desired consistency is reached.
4. Scrape the bottom of the bowl and mix on medium-high speed until all the ingredients are combined and the frosting is fluffy, about 2 minutes.

Coconut Strawberry Lemonade Cake

At last, all of these wonderful flavors coming together as one! The fresh sweetness of the strawberry frosting matches perfectly with the tart lemon curd. And all atop our coveted coconut cake. Pure heaven in your kitchen.

Makes one 9-inch round two-layer cake or 18 cupcakes

FOR THE COCONUT CAKE

3 cups (15 ounces) all-purpose flour

1 1/2 teaspoons baking powder

1/4 teaspoon salt

1 1/2 cups (10.5 ounces) sugar

2/3 cup non-hydrogenated vegan margarine (recommended: Earth Balance)

1/4 teaspoon almond extract

1/4 teaspoon coconut extract

2 teaspoons egg replacer (recommended: Ener-G)

2 tablespoons water

1 cup soymilk

3/4 cup coconut milk (recommended: So Delicious)

1 cup shredded dried unsweetened coconut, preferably desiccated

Lemon Curd (recipe follows)

Strawberry Frosting (recipe follows)

1. Preheat the oven to 350°F.
2. Line two 9-inch round cake pans with parchment paper, or lightly oil and dust with flour.
3. Whisk the flour, baking powder, and salt into a medium bowl. Set the bowl aside.
4. In the bowl of an electric stand mixer, combine the sugar, margarine, and almond and coconut extracts and cream with the whisk attachment, about 5 minutes. Scrape down the sides and bottom of the bowl to ensure that all the ingredients are combined.
5. In a small bowl or cup, combine the egg replacer and water and stir to

dissolve the egg replacer. Add the egg replacer to the sugar mixture and mix until combined. Scrape the bottom of the bowl to ensure that all the ingredients are combined.

6. In a small bowl, combine the soymilk and coconut milk and set aside.

7. Turn the mixer speed to low and slowly add the dry ingredients and the soymilk mixture, alternating between the two and ending with the soymilk. Be sure not to overmix the batter!

8. Fold the coconut in by hand, being careful not to overmix the batter.

9. Distribute the batter evenly between the two pans. Bake for 18 to 25 minutes, until a toothpick inserted in the middle comes out clean or the cake springs back to the touch.

10. Place the pans on a cooling rack to cool completely, then run a knife or plastic dough scraper around the edges of the pans to loosen the cakes from the sides. Turn the pans upside down to remove the cakes.

11. If you are making cupcakes, fill 18 lined cupcake cups three-quarters full and bake for 16 to 19 minutes, until a toothpick inserted in the center comes out clean. Place the cupcake tins on a cooling rack to cool completely, then turn the pans upside down to remove the cupcakes.

12. If you are making the layer cake, fill with the lemon curd, according to the instructions on page 26. Frost with the strawberry frosting. See pages 22–25 for prepping and frosting techniques.

VARIATION

You might also try kiwi curd (page 103) or blueberry frosting (page 97).

Lemon Curd

Makes about 2 cups

2 cups lemon juice

1 cup (7 ounces) sugar

¼ cup water

2 tablespoons egg replacer

6 tablespoons silken tofu

3 ½ tablespoons cornstarch

1. In a medium heavy-bottomed saucepan, heat the lemon juice and ½ cup of the sugar over medium heat, stirring until the sugar dissolves.
2. In a blender or food processor, combine the water, egg replacer, tofu, cornstarch, and the remaining ½ cup sugar and puree until smooth.
3. Add the tofu mixture to the saucepan with the hot lemon juice and bring to a boil.
4. Continue to cook, whisking, until the mixture becomes very thick, about 5 minutes.
5. Pour the hot mixture into a container and let rest at room temperature until cooled. Cover and refrigerate for at least 2 hours before using.

Strawberry Frosting

The scent of real strawberries and pure vanilla blended together in this smooth frosting smells better than any bouquet I've ever known.

Makes enough to frost one 9-inch round two-layer cake or 18 cupcakes

1 cup plus 2 tablespoons non-hydrogenated vegetable shortening (recommended: Earth Balance)

¼ cup plus 2 tablespoons non-hydrogenated vegan margarine (recommended: Earth Balance)

¾ cup strawberry puree, store-bought or homemade (see Note, page 40)

4 ½ cups (1 pound, 4 ounces) powdered sugar

1 teaspoon vanilla extract

1 ½ tablespoons lemon juice

1. In the bowl of a stand mixer, combine the shortening and margarine and whip with the paddle attachment until completely combined. Scrape the bottom of the bowl to ensure that the ingredients are mixed thoroughly.
2. Add the strawberry puree and mix until incorporated. Scrape the bottom of the bowl to ensure that all the ingredients are incorporated.

3. On low speed, slowly add the powdered sugar a little at a time.

4. Add the vanilla and lemon juice and mix to combine. Scrape the bottom of the bowl and mix on medium-high speed until all the ingredients are combined and the frosting is fluffy, about 2 minutes.

Love Bite

Medium-Chain Fatty Acids

Medium-chain fatty acids (MCFAs) are just one of the coconut's wonderful components. MCFAs are very easily digested and actually act more like carbohydrates than fats in our bodies. Our bodies can easily break them down and use them as energy immediately, rather than sticking to our hips and saving them for later. Where else can you find MCFAs? In human breast milk, that's where. No wonder it's regularly used in baby formulas to help mimic mama's milk.

Bunny Hugger's Carrot Cake

The best vehicle yet for getting your recommended daily dose of carrots. P.S.: You can also substitute other fabulous treats, such as raisins, dried ginger, or pecans for the walnuts. Go ahead and experiment. Design the next carrot cake classic!

Makes one 9-inch round two-layer cake or 18 cupcakes

oh, yummy moist!! no walnuts pls per Ba

2 cups grated carrots
½ cup (3.5 ounces) sugar
⅓ cup plus 1 ½ tablespoons (3 ounces) lightly packed brown sugar
1 teaspoon vanilla extract
¾ cup soymilk
⅔ cup canola or vegetable oil
1 ¼ cups plus 3 tablespoons (7.2 ounces) all-purpose flour
¾ cup (3.5 ounces) whole wheat pastry flour
1 teaspoon baking powder
1 teaspoon baking soda
¼ teaspoon salt
1 teaspoon ground cinnamon
¼ teaspoon ground allspice
½ cup walnuts, chopped or halved (optional)
Cream Cheese Frosting (page 48)

1. Preheat the oven to 350°F.
2. Line two 9-inch round cake pans with parchment paper, or lightly oil and dust with flour.
3. In a large bowl, mix together the carrots, sugars, and vanilla.
4. Add the soymilk and oil and stir to combine.
5. In a separate bowl, whisk together the flours, baking powder, baking soda, salt, cinnamon, and allspice. Toss the walnuts into the dry ingredients, if using. Add the dry ingredients to the wet ingredients and mix until just incorporated. The batter should be slightly lumpy.

6. Distribute the batter evenly between the two pans and bake for 20 minutes, or until the cakes spring back to the touch.

7. Place the pans on a cooling rack to cool completely, then run a knife or plastic dough scraper around the edges of the pans to loosen the cakes from the sides. Turn the pans upside down to remove the cakes.

8. If you are making cupcakes, fill 18 lined cupcake cups three-quarters full and bake for 16 to 19 minutes, until a toothpick inserted in the center comes out clean. Place the cupcake tins on a cooling rack to cool completely, then turn the pans upside down to remove the cupcakes.

9. Frost with the cream cheese frosting (see pages 22–25 for prepping and frosting techniques).

CHAT BREAK

This recipe started out as my own personal wedding cake. As I searched for a great wedding cake recipe to bring to our caterers, one that would satisfy a family filled with generations of meat eaters while holding up in the heat of Austin in August, I stumbled upon this cake in the bakery case at Wheatsville Market. It had a "vegan" sticker that caught my eye (this was the 1990s and Texas, so I thought they were mocking me). I took a detour from the cookbooks I had been looking through (to no avail) and feasted on the most delicious carrot cake. Not since I was a kid had I tasted such a sweet and moist carrot cake. I took the salesperson aside and told him the deal. I offered him five dollars to get me the recipe as I handed him a pencil, a piece of receipt paper, and a crisp new five-dollar bill. Five minutes later I had myself a cake recipe, the first version of our Bunny Hugger's Carrot Cake. Ten years later (happily married, I might add), we have an even better version (sans raisins) of the cake I tried that day and a much simpler recipe to navigate. Do I hear wedding bells?

Happy Hour: ID Required!

Piña Colada Cake

Let's face it, pineapple and coconut always taste great in tandem, and a little booze brings out the flavor, making it more fun to devour. Two-drink minimum!

Makes one 9-inch two-layer cake or 18 cupcakes

Coconut Cake (page 63)
Piña Colada Frosting (recipe follows)

1. Make the cake according to the instructions on pages 63–64. Cool completely, then wrap in plastic and refrigerate before frosting, as the frosting is quite soft. Frost with the piña colada frosting (see pages 22–25 for prepping and frosting techniques).

Piña Colada Frosting

Makes enough to frost one 9-inch round two-layer cake or 18 cupcakes

1 cup non-hydrogenated vegetable shortening (recommended: Earth Balance)

6 cups (1 pound, 11 ounces) powdered sugar

3 ½ teaspoons lemon juice

½ cup pineapple juice

1 ½ tablespoons light rum

¾ teaspoon coconut rum

1. In the bowl of a stand mixer, whip the shortening with the paddle
   attachment until completely softened. Scrape the bottom of the bowl.
2. On low speed, slowly add the powdered sugar a little at a time.
3. Once the sugar is incorporated, on low speed, slowly add the lemon juice,
   pineapple juice, and rums and mix until the liquids are incorporated.
4. Scrape the bottom of the bowl and mix on medium-high speed until all the
   ingredients are combined and the frosting is fluffy, about 2 minutes.

Strawberry Margarita Cake

Shots, anyone? Salt the rim of your cupcake by rolling the edge of the frosted cutie in a plate with sea salt, or sprinkle it along the edge of your cake. For more color and flare, use a fancy salt like pink or black salt.

Makes one 9-inch round two-layer cake or 18 cupcakes

2 ¾ cups plus 1 ½ tablespoons (14 ounces) all-purpose flour

1 tablespoon baking powder

½ teaspoon salt

1 ¼ cups plus 3 tablespoons (10 ounces) sugar

2/3 cup non-hydrogenated vegan margarine (recommended: Earth Balance)

1 ½ teaspoons egg replacer (recommended: Ener-G)

¼ cup water

½ cup finely chopped strawberries

¼ cup unsweetened strawberry puree, store-bought or homemade (see Note, page 40)

¾ cup soymilk

2 teaspoons vanilla extract

Margarita Frosting (recipe follows)

1. Preheat the oven to 350°F.
2. Line two 9-inch round cake pans with parchment paper, or lightly oil and dust with flour.
3. Whisk the flour, baking powder, and salt into a medium bowl. Set the bowl aside.
4. In the bowl of an electric stand mixer, combine the sugar and margarine, and cream together with the whisk attachment, about 5 minutes. Scrape down the sides and bottom of the bowl to ensure that the ingredients are incorporated.

5. In a small bowl or cup, combine the egg replacer and water and stir to dissolve the egg replacer. Add the egg replacer mixture to the sugar mixture and mix until combined. Scrape the bottom of the bowl to ensure that the ingredients are incorporated.

6. Add the strawberries and strawberry puree and mix until well combined. Scrape the bottom of the bowl.

7. In a small bowl, combine the soymilk and vanilla and set aside.

8. Turn the mixer speed to low and slowly add the dry ingredients and the soymilk mixture, alternating between the two and ending with the soymilk.

9. Distribute the batter evenly between the two pans. Bake for 18 to 25 minutes, until a toothpick inserted in the middle comes out clean or the cake springs back to the touch.

10. Place the pans on a cooling rack to cool completely, then run a knife or plastic dough scraper around the edges of the pans to loosen the cakes from the sides. Turn the pans upside down to remove the cakes.

11. If you are making cupcakes, fill 18 lined cupcake cups three-quarters full and bake for 16 to 19 minutes, until a toothpick inserted in the center comes out clean. Place the cupcake tins on a cooling rack to cool completely, then turn the tins upside down to remove the cupcakes.

12. Frost with the margarita frosting (see pages 22–25 for prepping and frosting techniques).

Margarita Frosting

Makes enough to frost one 9-inch round two-layer cake or 18 cupcakes

¾ cup non-hydrogenated vegetable shortening (recommended: Earth Balance)

7 ½ cups (2 pounds, 2 ounces) powdered sugar

¾ teaspoon salt

3 tablespoons tequila

⅓ cup plus 1 tablespoon lime juice

Yellow and green food coloring (optional)

1. In the bowl of a stand mixer, whip the shortening with the paddle attachment until completely softened. Scrape the bottom of the bowl.
2. On low speed, slowly add the powdered sugar a little at a time, then add the salt.
3. Once the sugar and salt are incorporated, add the tequila and lime juice and mix on low speed until the liquids are incorporated.
4. Scrape the bottom of the bowl and mix on medium-high speed until all the ingredients are combined and the frosting is fluffy, about 2 minutes.
5. Add one or two drops each of yellow and green food coloring, if using, and mix until incorporated.

Love Bite

Tequila

There are health benefits to be had by drinking tequila. Really, there are. It's a proven relaxant, it helps reduce cholesterol, and it aids digestion. While I'm pretty sure you can get the same benefits by going for a brisk walk, that wouldn't be nearly as fun or delicious.

However, if once upon a time during a particularly difficult breakup or especially exciting happy hour you managed to ruin yourself with the stuff, I have the cure: This frosting is magical and will reintroduce tequila to your life, but in a much more sobering and enjoyable manner. Combined with the heart-healthy benefits of strawberries—so good for the heart they are even shaped like one—you'll be ahead of the game.

The Manhattan

Chocolate whiskey cake and vermouth frosting make this pair as perfect as the cocktail it's named after. I love Manhattans, the warming whiskey spicy and smooth, accentuated by the vermouth. We've added a bit of cardamom and cinnamon to bring out the flavors that make vermouth spectacular.

Makes one 9-inch round two-layer cake or 18 cupcakes

1 ¼ cups soymilk

1 cup (4 ounces) cocoa powder

1 cup non-hydrogenated vegan margarine (recommended: Earth Balance)

¾ cup whiskey

1 cup (7 ounces) sugar

1 cup (7 ounces) brown sugar

2 cups (10 ounces) all-purpose flour

1 ½ teaspoons baking soda

½ teaspoon salt

3 tablespoons egg replacer (recommended: Ener-G)

⅓ cup water

Vermouth Frosting (recipe follows)

Maraschino cherries or orange twists for topping

1. Preheat the oven to 350°F.
2. Line two 9-inch round cake pans with parchment paper, or lightly oil and dust with flour.
3. In a medium heavy-bottomed saucepan, add the soymilk, cocoa powder, margarine, and whiskey.
4. Heat over medium heat, whisking, until the margarine is melted and the ingredients are incorporated.
5. Add the sugars and stir until they are dissolved. Remove from the heat.
6. Whisk the flour, baking soda, and salt into a large bowl and set aside.
7. In a small bowl, whisk together the egg replacer and water.
8. Add the soymilk mixture and egg replacer to the dry ingredients and whisk until just incorporated. Do not overmix the batter.

9. Distribute the batter evenly between the two pans. Bake for 18 to 25 minutes, until a toothpick inserted in the middle comes out clean or the cake springs back to the touch.

10. Place the pans on a cooling rack to cool completely, then run a knife or plastic dough scraper around the edges of the pans to loosen the cakes from the sides. Turn the pans upside down to remove the cakes.

11. If you are making cupcakes, fill 18 lined cupcake cups three-quarters full and bake for 16 to 19 minutes, until a toothpick inserted into a cupcake comes out clean. Place the cupcake tins on a cooling rack to cool completely, then turn the tins upside down to remove the cupcakes.

12. Frost with the vermouth frosting (see pages 22–25 for prepping and frosting techniques).

13. Top with a maraschino cherry or an orange twist.

Vermouth Frosting

Makes enough to frost one 9-inch round two-layer cake or 18 cupcakes

1 cup non-hydrogenated vegetable shortening (recommended: Earth Balance)

1 cup non-hydrogenated vegan margarine (recommended: Earth Balance)

4 cups (1 pound, 2 ounces) powdered sugar

¼ teaspoon ground cardamom

¼ teaspoon ground cinnamon

4 tablespoons sweet vermouth

Soymilk, if needed

1. In the bowl of a stand mixer, combine the shortening and margarine and whip until completely combined. Scrape the bottom of the bowl to ensure that the ingredients are mixed thoroughly.

2. On low speed, slowly add the powdered sugar, cardamom, and cinnamon a little at a time.

3. Once the sugar is incorporated, add the vermouth and mix on low speed until incorporated.

4. Scrape the bottom of the bowl and mix on medium-high speed until all the ingredients are combined and the frosting is fluffy, about 2 minutes.

5. If the frosting is too stiff, add a little soymilk, 1 tablespoon at a time, until the desired consistency is reached.

Chocolate Stout Cake

The only thing better than chocolate and chocolate is beer and chocolate. Stout acts in much the same way to chocolate as coffee does—it picks up the flavor and adds aromatic undertones that draw you in. Imbibe!

Makes one 9-inch round two-layer cake or 18 cupcakes

1 ¾ cups (8.75 ounces) all-purpose flour

1 ½ cups (10.5 ounces) sugar

½ cup (2 ounces) cocoa powder

1 teaspoon baking soda

½ teaspoon salt

1 cup water

½ cup stout beer

½ cup vegetable or canola oil

1 teaspoon vanilla extract

1 tablespoon vinegar (recommended: apple cider vinegar)

Vanilla Frosting (page 50)

Stout Ganache (recipe follows)

1. Preheat the oven to 350°F.
2. Line two 9-inch round cake pans with parchment paper, or lightly oil and dust with flour.
3. Whisk the flour, sugar, cocoa powder, baking soda, and salt into a medium bowl. Set the bowl aside.
4. In a small bowl, whisk together the water, stout, oil, and vanilla.
5. Add the wet ingredients to the dry ingredients and whisk until just incorporated.
6. Fold in the vinegar until you begin to see streaks. See Note on page 28 for reference. Do not overmix the batter.
7. Distribute the batter evenly between the two pans. Bake for 20 to 25 minutes, until the cakes spring back to the touch.
8. Place the pans on a cooling rack to cool completely, then run a knife or plastic dough scraper around the edges of the pans to loosen the cakes from the sides. Turn the pans upside down to remove the cakes.

9. If you are making cupcakes, fill 18 lined cupcake cups three-quarters full and bake for 16 to 19 minutes, until a toothpick inserted in the center comes out clean. Place the cupcake tins on a cooling rack to cool completely, then turn the tins upside down to remove the cupcakes.

10. Frost your cake with the vanilla frosting (see pages 22–25 for prepping and frosting techniques). A bottom border is fine, but leave off the top border.

11. Make sure your ganache is pourable but not hot to the touch, as you don't want to melt your frosting. With a spoon or a glass measuring pitcher, pour the ganache in the center of the cake until it reaches the sides. Pour a small amount along the edge, enough so you get a few drips running over the sides. Let the ganache set before moving the cake around or you risk losing your frosting and your ganache in a topping avalanche.

12. If you are making cupcakes, frost them however you like, with a round or star tip, or even by hand. Then fill a piping bag one-quarter full with ganache, cut a small part of the tip off, and drizzle the ganache over the cupcake. More chocolate is what you desire? Dip the entire top of the frosted cupcake into the ganache.

Stout Ganache

Makes 1 ½ cups

½ cup coconut creamer (recommended: So Delicious)
8 ounces 70% dark chocolate, chopped or pistoles
½ cup stout beer

1. Heat the coconut creamer in the top part of a double boiler over medium heat until steaming. Do not boil.

2. Place the chocolate in a heatproof bowl and pour the hot creamer over the chocolate; let sit for 30 seconds.

3. Whisk the stout and chocolate mixture until the chocolate is melted and the three ingredients are completely combined and the ganache is thick but still pourable.

Love Bite

Alcohol

The benefits from alcohol don't stop at red wine: Any alcoholic beverage will slow down your heart rate so you can relax at the end of a stressful day. Some believe the benefits in stout are astounding, and that there are antioxidant qualities in the dark and handsome brew. Will aspirin be replaced with a cold one to reduce the risk of killer clots and artery cloggers? What about cupcakes made with stout? Could we be onto something here?

Champagne Cake

Cheers! The bubbles from the champagne in this cake will make you giggle with glee when you take your first bite. The subtle white wine flavor is delicate and divine; the raspberries give it a bit of pomp and circumstance. And the frosting takes this cake over the top. I had never tasted passion fruit before. I mean, maybe in the form of a Tropical Skittle or the like, but never in the flesh. Not until we were filming for *Cupcake Wars* and Jenny, Sticky Fingers' head baker and my right-hand lady, cut a fruit open and spooned the innards into my mouth. What happened next? I will let you know this—it didn't make it past the edits.

Makes one 9-inch round two-layer cake or 18 cupcakes

2 ¾ cups (13.75 ounces) all-purpose flour

2 ½ teaspoons baking powder

½ teaspoon salt

1 ⅔ cups (11.8 ounces) sugar

½ cup non-hydrogenated vegan margarine (recommended: Earth Balance)

1 teaspoon vanilla extract

2 teaspoons egg replacer (recommended: Ener-G)

¾ cup soymilk

¾ cup champagne or sparkling white wine

2 pints fresh raspberries

Passion Fruit Frosting (recipe follows)

1. Preheat the oven to 350°F.
2. Line two 9-inch round cake pans with parchment paper.
3. Whisk the flour, baking powder, and salt into a medium bowl. Set the bowl aside.
4. In the bowl of an electric stand mixer, combine the sugar and margarine, and cream together with the whisk attachment, about 5 minutes. Scrape down the sides and bottom of the bowl to ensure that the ingredients are incorporated.

5. In a small bowl or cup, combine the egg replacer, vanilla, and soymilk and stir to dissolve the egg replacer.

6. Add the champagne to the soymilk mixture and mix until combined.

7. Turn the mixer speed to low and slowly add the dry ingredients and soymilk mixture, alternating between the two and ending with the dry ingredients.

8. Gently fold in the raspberries by hand, being careful not to break them.

9. Distribute the batter evenly between the two pans. Bake for 18 to 25 minutes, until a toothpick inserted in the middle comes out clean or the cake springs back to the touch.

10. Place the pans on a cooling rack to cool completely, then run a knife or plastic dough scraper around the edges of the pans to loosen the cakes from the sides. Turn the pans upside down to remove the cakes.

11. If you are making cupcakes, fill 18 lined cupcake cups three-quarters full and insert 1 raspberry in the center of each cupcake, making sure the batter covers the top of the raspberry. Bake for 16 to 19 minutes, until a toothpick inserted into a cupcake comes out clean. Place the cupcake tins on a cooling rack to cool completely, then turn the tins upside down to remove the cupcakes.

12. Frost with the passion fruit frosting (see pages 22–25 for prepping and frosting techniques). Top with fresh raspberries.

Passion Fruit Frosting

Makes enough to frost one 9-inch round two-layer cake or 18 cupcakes

1 ¼ cups non-hydrogenated vegetable shortening (recommended: Earth Balance)

¾ cup non-hydrogenated vegan margarine (recommended: Earth Balance)

½ cup passion fruit concentrate or puree

3 ½ cups (15.75 ounces) powdered sugar

1. In the bowl of a stand mixer, combine the shortening and margarine and whip until completely combined. Scrape the bottom of the bowl to ensure that all ingredients are mixed thoroughly.

2. Add the passion fruit concentrate or puree and mix until incorporated. Scrape the bottom of the bowl.

3. On low speed, slowly add the powdered sugar a little at a time.

4. Scrape the bottom of the bowl and mix on medium-high speed until all the ingredients are combined and the frosting is fluffy, about 2 minutes.

Love Bite

Champagne

Do the bubbles go straight to your head? Do you lose all control? Does your heart go a-flutter while you get all giddy inside? Me, too, and I don't even have to drink it. I use champagne in cake because it gives a unique flavor and a great pop when it goes into the oven. It's especially nice with fruit and citrus. Yes, flat liquids work just fine, but extra bubbles are better. Next time you celebrate, save the champagne for your cakes and cupcakes!

Chapter 3

Sticky Fingers' Signature Cupcakes

Cake is great, but cupcakes are cuter! The cupcake craze hasn't slowed down a bit, and here at Sticky Fingers we're just getting started. Cupcake makers, get ready to indulge and enjoy as we take on the task of creating this international sensation, vegan style!

Here we go—your chance to learn some handy tricks of the trade for making your cupcakes look like they spent hours at a salon. Your guests will be so impressed when you tell them you can decorate like a pro and then produce the goods to prove it.

Decorating Cupcakes

I know, you're thinking, "What's to know? Just spread some frosting on top, right?" Yes, the best cupcakes are just like that, an enormous dollop of fluffy frosting smeared on top of your fresh-baked cuppies. But I'll teach you some new techniques to incorporate fillings and toppings so that you can make cupcakes better than Martha Stewart. She won't have nothin' on you.

Let's start with piping. For piped cupcake tops, you'll need a frosting bag, a coupler (if you wish), and some frosting tips. There are lots of different tips to choose from, but in the Sticky Fingers kitchen, we have two kinds that we use most often for cupcakes: the large star and the large round. The large star tip makes a really nice fluted swirl on top of your cupcake, perfect for catching drizzled toppings like caramel and melted chocolate. The large round tip is great for making a fluffy dollop on top of your cupcakes. Just keep in mind that stars and rounds come in different sizes, so make sure you get the really big ones for your cupcakes (the smaller versions are great for piping details on cakes).

So get that frosting bag ready! Place your coupler (if using) inside the bag, snip the end, and attach your tip. If you don't have a coupler, just put your tip right inside the bag and snip the end so your tip won't pop out and the plastic is out of the way. No tips? Then simply snip the end of your bag about 1/4 inch wide. Fill your frosting bag about three-quarters full, place the bag between your thumb and forefinger, and twist the top to make sure none escapes out the back hatch. Squeeze a little back into your frosting container to get the air bubbles out. In order to get that nice uniform fluffy tuft atop each cupcake, you can follow our quick and easy method:

1. Start with your frosting bag directly over your cupcake.
2. Place the tip about 1/2 inch away from the surface at two o'clock.
3. Now, holding the bag upright, move the tip counterclockwise around the cupcake while putting lots of pressure on your frosting bag.
4. Swing it all the way back around just past your starting position and pull it into the center for a nice finish.

You want to squeeze the frosting bag with your right hand (or left, depending on your persuasion) just above the twist so you have maximum control. Make sure you put enough pressure on your frosting bag so that the frosting really does the work for you. You are just guiding it along with a minor hand movement. You can rest your left hand on the bag to help stabilize your motions. If you need more help, you can visit our YouTube channel, Stickyfingersdc, for a demo—come hang out with us!

Okay, let's move on to fillings. Who doesn't love memories of those creamy filled cupcakes, neatly packaged and eternally shelf stable? You remember the ones I'm talking about, the cupcakes with the pillow of frosting seemingly magically baked inside? Well, you can make those even better! All you have to do is make some space for that creamy goodness to nest in. We use a big round frosting tip to make a hole in the center of our cupcakes. Just take the tip and press it down into the center of your cupcake and there you have a perfect little space to squeeze your filling into. No tip? Cut a little bit out of the center, or better yet, any finger will do. Then put your filling into a frosting bag to make the work a little faster (and to fill that cupcake to maximum capacity), or you can use a spoon to fill 'em up. Just be careful not to overfill your cupcakes. If the edges start to bulge or the top starts to crack, stop squeezing!

If you really want to replicate that store-bought cream-filled cupcake, you'll want to coat the top of your cupcake in ganache. When using ganache for cupcakes, make sure that the ganache is thin enough to pour rather than thick and spreadable. Take your cupcake and dip the top into the ganache. Hold it above the bowl for a second so that the excess can drizzle back down into the bowl. Let it rest so the ganache can set, just a minute or two. You can give it a double dunk if you want the ganache to be nice and thick. If you plan to put frosting on top after it is covered in chocolaty goodness, make sure that you let the ganache set completely before piping on your frosting, at least 20 minutes. Otherwise your frosting will just slide right off!

Okay, so now that you have filling, ganache dipping, and piping down, you can get creative with your toppings! Drizzle some caramel or melted chocolate for a really decadent look, or add a piece of fruit that complements your flavors. Chocolate chips or coffee beans are good toppers for the right flavors, and marshmallows are a welcome touch. Of course, sprinkles are always festive, and you can pipe on frosting flowers if you really want to get crazy! You can even roll your frosted treats in chocolate shavings, cookie crumbs, coconut, or nuts (really, anything crunchy will do), or add a little cocktail umbrella for a fancy flair. Let your inner Martha go nuts (with nuts!) and play around with your flavors.

The No'Stess with the Mostess Cupcake

No need to miss those childhood treats. No need to be sad when you pass the snack-pack aisle—we've got a memory-lane cupcake especially for you!

Makes 18 cupcakes

Chocolate Love Cake (page 29)
Vanilla Frosting (page 50)
Chocolate Ganache (page 41)

1. Make the cupcakes according to the instructions on page 29.
2. Make the vanilla frosting (see page 50) to fill the cupcakes. Use a large round frosting tip to make a hole in the center of your cupcakes. Take the tip and press it down into the center of your cupcake to make space to squeeze your filling into.
3. Put your filling into a frosting bag and cut about ½ inch off the tip. Be careful not to overfill your cupcakes. If the edges start to bulge or the top starts to crack, stop squeezing!
4. Make the ganache according to the directions on page 41. Take your cupcake and dip the top into the ganache. Hold it up, ganache-side down, above the bowl for a second so that the excess can drizzle back down.
5. Set the cupcake aside and let it set up for a few minutes. You can give it a double dunk if you want the ganache to be nice and thick.
6. If you plan to put frosting on top after it is topped with ganache, let the ganache set completely before piping on your frosting—at least 20 minutes. Otherwise, your frosting will slide right off.
7. Using a piping bag fitted with a number 3, 4, or 5 round tip, pipe loops across each cupcake with your vanilla frosting.

Our Prize-Winning Cupcakes!

Wanna know how we got on TV? Wanna know how it all happened? Play by play, here it goes: We got a phone call one day from *Cupcake Wars*. What? Why? We didn't ask to be on a reality TV show; we had a store to run and an empire to build! So when they asked us to apply, my first reaction was "I'm busy!" My second reaction, as the competitive Doron pushed through to rear her big ole self, was "When do you need the audition video?" The next day we had one ready and sent it off. No, it's not on YouTube. It's filled with inappropriate references and language. And there may or may not be nudity. Don't judge.

A week later, Jenny Webb and I were asked to join in the insanity. We memorized our recipes and techniques, started practicing our decorating, and learned some new tricks. We had to go there with our minds filled with nothing except cupcake know-how.

The morning we got there, one of the producers asked me how I felt and if I was ready. I put my game face on and furrowed my brow. "Let's go," I said, and that became my mantra throughout the show.

Standing in front of the judges for the first time, we learned the task at hand. Using at least two of the ingredients presented to us, we had to come up with a funny flavor that would fit a high-profile event with a rather witty guest list. Hardly an item on hand was vegan, but as I scanned the ingredient table I saw the two I could use: banana and seltzer water, which we used to create a chocolate seltzer cupcake topped with ganache, banana frosting, and caramelized bananas. I daftly named it the Gilbert Ganachefried cupcake. Round one was in the bag. Edited out of that round was a judge saying, "I know you are a vegan bakery, but I thought this was real banana cream." I nearly cried.

Round two proved to be more difficult, as the competition became more intense. We were challenged to come up with three more silly crowd pleasers, all to be served at the infamous Ice House 50th Anniversary Party. The funniest of the funny folks would be there, and we had to style cupcakes to make them laugh.

Jenny and I thought of flavor combos on the fly and matching names as well. The mix: Working Blue, a ginger cake with peach-brandy filling, blueberry frosting, and a talking blueberry on top; Strawberry Daiq-kiwi, vanilla cake filled with kiwi curd and topped with strawberry frosting and a rum-filled strawberry; and the George Caramelin (our ode to George Carlin), chocolate spice cupcakes filled with bourbon caramel, topped with bourbon and vanilla bean frosting, slathered in more of the caramel, and decorated with candied pecans. Our "sludge-like" ganache (you can do better with less pressure!) nearly lost us the round, but our unique and cheeky presentation kept us in the game. We made it through and I kicked it into overdrive. The adrenaline pumping through our veins was well over the legal limit and we had to move fast.

Quickly, Jenny began making the one thousand cupcakes with the group of assistants, and I began designing the display to hold the one thousand comical cuppies to be showcased at the Ice House event that night. The pressure was on and our cupcake lives were at stake. I came up with an igloo design for the display, and the carpenters began their work. Jenny was a gem and completely stone-cold rocked it each and every round. She was my rock, my muse, and by the end of the day she was so tired of the high fives and cheerleader Doron (yes, I was a cheerleader in high school—that's a whole other book) that she nearly kicked me out of the kitchen. You may have missed the part when she starts yelling at me to "Calm the 'f' down and focus."

And there we were, at the last round, standing in front of the judges for what seemed like forever. I began to retrace the day and question my moves. Did we lose it on the ganache? Were we funny enough? And then I heard my name, followed by the words "You are this *Cupcake Wars'* winner." My NYC roots came rushing back into me quicker than I could catch them, and what erupted next was staggering: fist pumps. The George Caramelin. Gilbert Ganachefried, Working Blue, and Strawberry Daiq-kiwi cupcakes were the key to our success! And now you can make these award-winning cupcakes in your own kitchen.

George Caramelin

Making the caramel sauce for this cupcake is no joke. Please follow the directions carefully and take precautions. Sugar at its boiling point gets upward of 300ºF, and it splatters a lot while hanging out there. Get yourself some good oven mitts that come up midarm. Put the dogs and cats in the other room and put the babies in their playpens. This could get messy, but you will thank me later.

Makes 18 cupcakes

FOR THE CHOCOLATE CINNAMON CAKE

1 ¾ cups plus 1 ½ tablespoons
   (9.2 ounces) all-purpose flour

1 ¼ cups plus 3 tablespoons
   (10 ounces) sugar

½ cup plus 2 teaspoons
   (2.2 ounces) cocoa powder

2 teaspoon ground cinnamon

2 teaspoons baking soda

½ teaspoon salt

1 ½ cups coconut milk
   (recommended: So Delicious)

2/3 cup vegetable or canola oil

½ cup brewed coffee,
   cooled

1 teaspoon vanilla extract

2 teaspoons vinegar

Vanilla Bean Bourbon Frosting
   (recipe follows)

Bourbon Caramel Sauce
   (recipe follows)

Candied Pecans (recipe
   follows)

1. Preheat the oven to 350ºF.
2. Whisk the flour, sugar, cocoa, cinnamon, baking soda, and salt into a medium bowl. Set the bowl aside.
3. In a small bowl, whisk together the coconut milk, oil, coffee, and vanilla.
4. Add the wet ingredients to the dry ingredients and whisk until just incorporated.

5. Fold in the vinegar until you begin to see streaks. See Note on page 28 for reference. Do not overmix the batter.

6. Fill 18 lined cupcake cups three-quarters full and bake for 16 to 19 minutes, until a toothpick inserted in the center comes out clean.

7. Place the cupcake tins on a cooling rack to cool completely, then turn the tins upside down to remove the cupcakes.

Vanilla Bean Bourbon Frosting

This is going to change the way you feel about bourbon. No bad memories of painful mornings after. This topping is going to make you a fan.

Makes enough frosting for 18 cupcakes

1 cup plus 2 tablespoons non-hydrogenated vegetable shortening (recommended: Earth Balance)

¼ cup plus 2 tablespoons non-hydrogenated vegan margarine (recommended: Earth Balance)

4 ½ cups (1 pound, 4 ounces) powdered sugar

½ teaspoon vanilla bean paste

4 tablespoons bourbon

1. In the bowl of a stand mixer, whip the shortening and margarine with the paddle attachment until completely combined. Scrape the bottom of the bowl to ensure that all ingredients are mixed thoroughly.

2. On low speed, slowly add the sugar a little at a time.

3. Once the sugar is incorporated, add the vanilla paste and bourbon, 1 tablespoon at a time, and mix on low until the liquids are incorporated.

4. Scrape the bottom of the bowl, and mix on medium-high speed until all ingredients are combined and frosting is fluffy, about 2 minutes.

Bourbon Caramel Sauce

Makes 2 cups

¼ cup vinegar or lemon juice

2 cups (14 ounces) sugar

½ cup water

⅔ cup bourbon

¼ teaspoon sea salt

2 teaspoons non-hydrogenated vegan margarine (recommended: Earth Balance)

1. Rinse out a small, heavy-bottomed saucepan, preferably stainless-steel, with the vinegar or lemon juice. This will help to remove any residue left behind that could interfere with the candying process.

2. In the saucepan, stir together the sugar and water.

3. Cover and bring to a boil.

4. Remove the lid and insert a candy thermometer.

5. Turn the heat down slightly and let the mixture boil until it starts to turn brown and just reaches the soft-ball stage (no more than 240ºF), about 20 minutes. Do not stir during this step!

6. Remove from the heat and stir with a whisk.

7. Add the bourbon and salt and continue stirring.

8. Once the bubbling stops, add the margarine and whisk until melted and distributed.

9. Let cool completely and pour into a clean squirt bottle or glass jar.

Candied Pecans

2 tablespoons non-hydrogenated
    vegan margarine
    (recommended: Earth
    Balance)

2 tablespoons dark brown
    sugar
½ teaspoon ground cinnamon
1 cup pecan halves or pieces

1. Place the margarine in a microwave-safe bowl and melt it in the microwave.
2. Stir in the brown sugar and cinnamon. The mixture will be slightly grainy.
3. Toss the pecans into the mixture and pour onto parchment paper or a baking sheet to cool and harden.

ASSEMBLY REQUIRED

Once your cupcakes are cooled, use a plastic drinking straw or a small paring knife to make holes in the center of each cupcake. Squeeze the cooled but pourable bourbon caramel sauce into the cupcake until it is filled but not overflowing, about 1 tablespoon per cupcake. Pipe a dollop of vanilla bean bourbon frosting on top of each cupcake. Drizzle the top with more bourbon caramel sauce and sprinkle with candied pecans to garnish. Voilà! A winning masterpiece.

Working Blue

This cupcake is like candy in your mouth. The zing of the ginger, the kick the brandy-peach filling gives, all smoothed over with bright blueberry frosting. Holy $%@#! This is a tasty cupcake!

Makes 18 cupcakes

FOR THE GINGER CAKE

2 ¾ cups plus 1 ½ tablespoons (14 ounces) all-purpose flour

1 tablespoon baking powder

½ teaspoon salt

1 ¼ cups plus 3 tablespoons (10 ounces) sugar

⅔ cup non-hydrogenated vegan margarine (recommended: Earth Balance)

1 ½ teaspoons egg replacer (recommended: Ener-G)

¼ cup plus 2 tablespoons water

½ cup packed minced ginger (about 6 ounces whole unpeeled ginger root)

2 tablespoons ginger juice, store-bought or freshly squeezed

¾ cup soymilk

2 teaspoons vanilla extract

Peach Filling (recipe follows)

Blueberry Frosting (recipe follows)

Fresh blueberries for topping

1. Preheat the oven to 350°F.
2. Whisk the flour, baking powder, and salt into a medium bowl. Set the bowl aside.
3. In the bowl of an electric stand mixer, combine the sugar and margarine and cream together with the whisk attachment, about 5 minutes. Scrape down the sides and bottom of the bowl to ensure that the ingredients are incorporated.
4. In a small bowl or cup, combine the egg replacer and water and stir to

dissolve the egg replacer. Add the egg replacer to the sugar mixture and mix until combined. Scrape the bottom of the bowl.

5. Add the ginger and ginger juice and mix until well combined. Scrape the bottom of the bowl.

6. In a small bowl, combine the soymilk and vanilla and set aside.

7. Turn the mixer speed to low and slowly add the dry ingredients and the soymilk, alternating between the two and ending with the soymilk.

8. Fill 18 lined cupcake cups three-quarters full and bake for 16 to 19 minutes, until a toothpick inserted in the center comes out clean.

9. Place the cupcake tins on a cooling rack to cool completely, then turn the tins upside down to remove the cupcakes.

Love Bite

....

Ginger

The ginger you're about to eat can work wonders you've never dreamed of. That lump of pink flaky bits alongside your cucumber rolls? Yes, exactly. Remember that bruise you got at your last race? Or that sore knee, the one that comes back to remind you of the day you fell on it ten years ago? Ginger can help. The anti-inflammatory effects of ginger are all-encompassing. So powerful yet gentle, its zestiness can soothe a colicky baby and temper a tumultuous tummy. I wouldn't advise feeding these cupcakes to a screaming infant, but they will definitely make you feel better.

Peach Filling

Makes about 2 cups

2 cups prepared peach puree, store-bought or homemade (see Note)
3 tablespoons sugar
1 tablespoon cornstarch
1 tablespoon brandy or water

1. In a medium, heavy-bottomed saucepan, combine the peach puree and sugar and stir over medium-high heat until bubbling.
2. In a small bowl, stir the cornstarch and brandy into a slurry.
3. Slowly whisk the cornstarch mixture into the puree mixture.
4. Cook for 2 more minutes, stirring, then remove from the heat and let cool completely.

NOTE

To make homemade peach puree, place 4 cups of peeled and roughly chopped fresh or frozen peaches (from 4 to 5 peaches) in a medium, heavy-bottomed saucepan. Place over medium-high heat and cook, stirring constantly, until they break down, about 15 minutes. Remove from heat and blend with an electric hand blender, then return to the heat and cook down until most of the liquid is evaporated, about 15 minutes. Let cool completely before using.

Blueberry Frosting

Makes enough to frost 18 cupcakes

1 cup plus 2 tablespoons non-hydrogenated vegetable shortening (recommended: Earth Balance)

¼ cup plus 2 tablespoons non-hydrogenated vegan margarine (recommended: Earth Balance)

½ cup blueberry puree, store-bought or homemade (see Note, page 40)

4 ½ cups (1 pound, 4 ounces) powdered sugar

1 ½ tablespoons blueberry juice concentrate

1 teaspoon vanilla extract

1. In the bowl of a stand mixer, combine the shortening and margarine and whip with the paddle attachment until completely combined. Scrape the bottom of the bowl to ensure that the ingredients are mixed thoroughly.
2. Add the blueberry puree and mix until incorporated. Scrape the bottom of the bowl.
3. On low speed, slowly add the powdered sugar a little at a time.
4. Add the blueberry juice and vanilla and mix to combine. Scrape the bottom of the bowl and mix on medium-high speed until all the ingredients are combined and the frosting is fluffy, about 2 minutes.

ASSEMBLY REQUIRED

Once your cupcake has cooled, cut holes in the center of each cupcake, using a spoon or knife. Using a piping bag or a spoon, fill the center with the puree, about 1 tablespoon. Use a round tip in a pastry bag or frost the top of your cupcake by hand. Pretty it up with a fresh blueberry.

Love Bite

Blueberries

Blueberries are total overachievers. They can do a little bit of everything, and they do it so well. They are low in calories, rich in antioxidants, and high in fiber, and they taste incredible. They save us from free radicals and toxins, feed us when we're hungry, and make everything they touch perfectly delicious. I'm almost jealous of how perfect they are.

Gilbert Ganachefried

The magic in this recipe is in picking the perfect banana—slightly green on each end, no black spots, barely ripe. This will keep your frosting from becoming slimy, and make it easy to whip and hold its fluffiness. The older the banana, the softer it is, as its cell walls break down with age. Tasty they may be when ripe, they are no good for making light and fluffy frosting.

Makes 18 cupcakes

FOR THE CHOCOLATE SELTZER CAKE

1 ¾ cups plus 1 ½ tablespoons (9.2 ounces) all-purpose flour

1 ½ cups plus 3 tablespoons (10 ounces) sugar

½ cup plus 3 tablespoons (2.7 ounces) cocoa powder

2 teaspoons baking soda

½ teaspoon salt

1 ½ cups seltzer water

2/3 cup canola or vegetable oil

½ cup brewed coffee, cooled

1 teaspoon vanilla extract

2 teaspoons vinegar (recommended: apple cider vinegar)

Chocolate Ganache (page 41)

Banana Frosting (recipe follows)

Caramelized Bananas (recipe follows)

1. Preheat the oven to 350°F.
2. Whisk the flour, sugar, cocoa powder, baking soda, and salt into a medium bowl. Set the bowl aside.
3. In a small bowl, whisk together the seltzer water, oil, coffee, and vanilla.
4. Add the wet ingredients to the dry ingredients and whisk until just incorporated.
5. Fold in the vinegar until you begin to see streaks. See Note on page 28 for reference. Do not overmix the batter.

6. Fill 18 lined cupcake cups three-quarters full and bake for 16 to 19 minutes, until a toothpick inserted in the center comes out clean. Place the cupcake tins on a cooling rack to cool completely, then turn the tins upside down to remove the cupcakes.

Banana Frosting

Makes enough to frost 18 cupcakes

1 cup plus 2 tablespoons non-hydrogenated vegetable shortening (recommended: Earth Balance)

¼ cup plus 2 tablespoons non-hydrogenated vegan margarine (recommended: Earth Balance)

3 ½ teaspoons vanilla extract

3 ¾ cups (1 pound, 1 ounce) powdered sugar

1 ½ slightly ripe bananas

3 to 6 tablespoons soymilk, as needed

1. In the bowl of a stand mixer, combine the shortening, margarine, and vanilla. Whip with the paddle attachment. Scrape the bottom of the bowl to ensure that all the ingredients are mixed thoroughly.

2. Slowly add the powdered sugar, a little at a time.

3. Once the powdered sugar is incorporated, mix on medium-high speed until all the ingredients are combined and the frosting is fluffy, about 2 minutes.

4. Drop the bananas into the frosting and continue mixing for an additional 2 minutes, or until the bananas are mashed and incorporated.

5. On low speed, add the soymilk a little at a time until incorporated and the desired consistency is reached.

Caramelized Bananas

¼ cup (1.75 oz) brown sugar

1 tablespoon non-hydrogenated margarine (recommended: Earth Balance)

2 large ripe bananas, sliced 1 inch thick

1 tablespoon rum

1. In a small saucepan, melt the brown sugar and margarine over medium heat. Once the sugar is completely melted, add the sliced bananas. Let the mixture come to a boil for 2 to 5 minutes, until the sauce thickens to the desired consistency.
2. Add the rum and stir, then remove from the heat and let cool.

ASSEMBLY REQUIRED

Once the cupcakes are cooled, dip the top of each cupcake in the smooth, warm but not hot ganache. Let the ganache cool and set. Pipe a dollop (a small one or a big one, depending on your level of sweet tooth) of banana frosting on top of the cupcake. Last, place two caramelized banana slices on top and drizzle some of their sauce on top as well. Enjoy!

Love Bite

....

Rum

Where would we be without rum? We'd be in a world of tired, hysterical, anemic pirates, that's where. If it weren't for rum, our lives would be void of drama-filled pirate stories and Johnny Depp would only ever be remembered as Edward Scissorhands rather than for his stellar performance in *Pirates of the Caribbean*. Rum was given to seamen to fight off scurvy, though the vitamin C–rich lime in the grog was probably what warded off the nasty ailment. The British Navy has been rationing a tot of rum to all enlisted people, including those on dry land, for ages. According to a very reputable inside source, the British Navy continues to do so, though you may now opt for a pint of ale if a shot is a bit much for you. The precaution is so enticing, I think it should be carried over from our British forefathers and deemed a national requirement for our health and well-being here in the States.

Strawberry Daiq-kiwi

This cupcake is insta-mouthwatering good.

Makes 18 cupcakes

Classic Vanilla Cake (page 49)
or Coconut Strawberry Lemonade
   Cake (page 63)
Kiwi Curd (recipe follows)

Strawberry Daiquiri Frosting
   (recipe follows)
All Cracked Up Strawberry Shot
   (recipe follows)

Make the cupcakes according to the instructions on page 49 or page 63.

Kiwi Curd

Kiwi can be enjoyed as a curd in a number of recipes to complement light and bright flavors. Zesty citrus or rich chocolate will overpower and ignore the kiwi, so match it with recipes from the lighter side, like vanilla, coconut, or strawberry.

Makes about 2 cups

2 cups kiwi puree (store-bought
   or homemade; see Note)
1 tablespoon lemon juice

1 cup (7 ounces) sugar
¼ cup water
¼ cup cornstarch

1. In a medium, heavy-bottomed saucepan, combine the kiwi puree, lemon juice, and sugar.
2. Heat over medium-high heat until the mixture begins to bubble around the edges.

3. In a small bowl, mix the water and cornstarch into a slurry.
4. Slowly whisk the cornstarch mixture into the kiwi mixture and cook, stirring, for 2 minutes. Remove from the heat and let cool completely.

NOTE

To make homemade kiwi puree, in a medium, heavy-bottomed saucepan, heat 4 cups peeled and roughly chopped fresh or frozen kiwis (10 to 12 kiwis) over medium-high heat, stirring constantly until they break down, about 15 minutes. Remove from the heat and blend with an electric hand blender. Return to the heat and cook down until most of the liquid is evaporated, about 15 minutes. Let cool completely before using.

Strawberry Daiquiri Frosting

Makes enough to frost 18 cupcakes

1 cup plus 2 tablespoons non-hydrogenated vegetable shortening (recommended: Earth Balance)

¼ cup plus 2 tablespoons non-hydrogenated vegan margarine (recommended: Earth Balance)

½ cup strawberry puree (store-bought or homemade; see Note, page 40)

4 ½ cups (1 pound, 4 ounces) powdered sugar

1 ½ tablespoons lemon juice

1 ½ tablespoons dark rum

1. In the bowl of a stand mixer, combine the shortening and margarine and whip with the paddle attachment until completely combined.
2. Scrape the bottom of the bowl to ensure that the ingredients are mixed thoroughly. Add the strawberry puree and mix until incorporated. Scrape the bottom of the bowl.

3. On low speed, slowly add the powdered sugar a little at a time.

4. Add the lemon juice and rum and mix to combine. Scrape the bottom of the bowl and mix on medium-high speed until all the ingredients are combined and the frosting is fluffy, about 2 minutes.

All Cracked Up Strawberry Shot

Shots, anyone? This is a super-fun garnish that really packs a punch for a truly adult cupcake. You will need a paring knife and a liquid dropper or squeeze bottle for this recipe.

Yield 18 strawberries

18 large strawberries
½ cup rum

Grab a strawberry. At the fattest width of the strawberry, pierce it diagonally from the top, taking care not to go through to the other side. At the bottom of that pierced line, in the opposite direction, pierce the strawberry again, making a V, and then again to make a W. Work your way around, making lots of Ws until you meet up with the first piercing. Remove the top of the strawberry and drop about 1 teaspoon of rum into the hollow bottom of each berry. Place a very small tip on a pastry bag (or fill a heavy-duty freezer bag and pierce open one of the corners) and pipe frosting on the top of each rum-filled strawberry. This is like your caulking, keeping the rum in the bottom of the berry. Then place the top back on, gently. Now, top your filled and frosted cupcake with your rum-filled strawberry.

ASSEMBLY REQUIRED

With a plastic drinking straw or a small paring knife, make holes in the center of each cupcake. Using a piping bag or spoon, fill the center of each cupcake with kiwi curd, about 1 tablespoon per cupcake. Pipe a dollop of the strawberry daiquiri frosting on top of each cupcake and garnish with a rum-filled strawberry.

Love Bite

....

Fruit

According to a study published in the *Archives of Ophthalmology*, "Eating three or more servings of fruit per day may lower your risk of age-related macular degeneration (ARMD), the primary cause of vision loss in older adults." I can't make this stuff up, people, trust me! Fruit can save your eyesight, and you have to start early. ARMD is reversible when caught early, but the painful eye injections may cause you to choose blindness over treatment. To save yourself, eat fruit, and lots of it! Kiwi is easy to devour because it's super-delicious, small, and portable. So if you're maxed out on the standards, let kiwi be your new standby.

Chapter 4

The Trifecta

The Three Recipes
That Built This Bakery

These are three recipes that built this bakery—still our best sellers today! There's no secret formula to the thought process behind them. No sudden revelation of what to make. No hand of god or burst of fate. I admit my muse, my inspiration, and my lust: Hostess and Little Debbie snack cakes. Don't judge—you know you ate enough to live off of at some point. No, I didn't create the oatmeal cream pie, the devil's food chocolate-covered cream-filled snack cake, or the cinnamon bun. But give me a teensy bit of credit—I did transform the mainstream versions, the lard-laden and trans-fat-trolling counterparts, into digestible and equally tasty vegan alternatives. No small task! However, it was not nearly as difficult and complicated as one would imagine. Go on, try it for yourself.

Cowvin Cookie

This is our most popular item at Sticky Fingers, and people travel from near and far to indulge in its divine goodness. Once I even received a blog post from a woman who was determined to unlock the secrets of the Cowvin and make them for herself. Her sad attempts at true bliss made me weep. I realized then the power of the Cowvin could not be denied. Eat one. You will be a devotee in no time.

Makes 10 to 12 cookies

½ cup non-hydrogenated vegan margarine (recommended: Earth Balance)

⅔ cup (4.6 ounces) sugar

¾ cup plus 2 ½ tablespoons (6.4 ounces) lightly packed brown sugar

1 teaspoon vanilla extract

¼ cup plus 1 tablespoon soymilk

¼ cup plus 1 tablespoon vegetable or canola oil

2 ½ cups (12 ounces) all-purpose flour

½ teaspoon baking powder

½ teaspoon baking soda

¼ teaspoon salt

1 ¾ cups rolled oats (not instant)

Creamy Vanilla Filling (recipe follows)

1. Preheat the oven to 350°F.
2. Line two baking sheets with parchment paper.
3. In the bowl of a stand mixer, combine the margarine, sugars, and vanilla, and cream together with the paddle attachment until light and fluffy, about 3 minutes. Scrape the bottom of the bowl to ensure that all the ingredients are mixed. Mix for 1 minute more to combine thoroughly.
4. In a small bowl, whisk together the soymilk and oil.
5. With the mixer running on low speed, slowly drizzle in the soymilk mixture.

Scrape the bowl again to make sure all the ingredients are mixed; mix for 1 minute more if necessary.

6. In a large bowl, whisk together the flour, baking powder, baking soda, and salt. Stir in the oats. Add the dry ingredients to the wet ingredients and mix until just combined.

7. Scoop the dough onto the baking sheets with a spring-loaded 2-ounce ice cream scoop. Leave 2 to 3 inches between each cookie and gently pat down with your fingertips.

8. Bake in the center rack of the oven for 9 to 11 minutes, or until the cookies appear dry on top.

9. Place the pan on a cooling rack and cool completely while you make the frosting.

10. Fill a pastry bag with the frosting and pipe a large dollop of frosting on the flat (bottom) side of half of the cookies. Top with the remaining cookies, flat side down, pressing down slightly so the filling spreads to the edges of the cookies.

Creamy Vanilla Filling

Makes 2 cups

¼ cup plus 2 tablespoons non-hydrogenated vegetable shortening (recommended: Earth Balance)

2 tablespoons non-hydrogenated vegan margarine (recommended: Earth Balance)

1 ⅓ cups (6.25 ounces) powdered sugar

1 teaspoon vanilla extract

½ to 1 tablespoon soymilk, as needed

1. In the bowl of a stand mixer, combine the shortening and margarine and whip with the paddle attachment until completely combined.

Scrape the bottom of the bowl to ensure that the ingredients are mixed thoroughly.

2. On low speed, slowly add the powdered sugar a little at a time.

3. Add the vanilla and then the soymilk, and mix on low speed until the liquids are incorporated and the desired consistency is reached. Scrape the bottom of the bowl and mix on medium-high speed until all the ingredients are combined and the frosting is fluffy, about 2 minutes. To make the frosting go further, let it whip a little longer, adding some air for lift.

CHAT BREAK

Cowvin. Pronounced like *Calvin* but with a *w* in place of the *l*. Cowvin was a tiny baby calf I had the pleasure of feeding one afternoon at a sanctuary in West Virginia. He was so small and had those big brown eyes, the ones that make you want to give up your last morsel of food. So I did. But something was wrong. He wasn't only tiny; his entire back was completely raw. I mean raw with droplets of blood at the surface of his flesh and not a bit of fur at all. The caretaker explained that when veal calves are in the crate, they can't swat the flies off of their backs, and their mommas aren't there to care for them. So they suffer. And he suffered. He was there eating as fast as he could and wincing from the pain. I had the pleasure of visiting Cowvin up until he was eight years old, when he passed from the bovine equivalent of old age. His favorite treats were oats, and he would run to his fence if he sensed anyone holding some. In his honor we created the Cowvin cookie: a cream-filled oat sandwich cookie people and cows go crazy for. It has a cult-like following of folks who travel far and wide to fill their need. I think it even has its own Facebook page.

Little Devils

The only thing missing from these lovely little mouthfuls of bliss is the thin foil wrapper I remember from once when. This is a completely selfish re-creation of one of my favorite bakery snacks from when I was a teen. They never get old, go out of style, or lose their zip. Still a best seller in our store today, these were my first try at treat re-creation. We cut ours into a handy 2 by 4-inch hand-held sweet. The prototypes were 4 by 4-inch squares. Preposterous, but I could eat the entire thing.

Makes 10 devils

2 2/3 cups (13.4 ounces) all-purpose flour

1/2 cup (2.6 ounces) whole wheat pastry flour

1 2/3 cups (11.5 ounces) sugar

1/2 cup (2 ounces) cocoa powder

1 tablespoon baking powder

1 teaspoon salt

1 3/4 cups water

2/3 cup vegetable or canola oil

1 tablespoon vanilla extract

2 tablespoons vinegar (recommended: apple cider vinegar)

1 cup chocolate chips

Creamy Vanilla Filling (page 111)

1. Preheat the oven to 350°F.
2. Line a 17 by 11-inch baking sheet or baking pan with parchment paper.
3. In a large bowl, combine the flours, sugar, cocoa powder, baking powder, and salt.
4. In a small bowl, whisk together the water, oil, and vanilla and add to the dry ingredients. Mix until the batter is smooth.
5. Fold in the vinegar until you begin to see streaks. See Note on page 28 for reference. Do not overmix the batter.
6. Pour the batter into the prepared pan and bake for 16 to 20 minutes, until the cake bounces back to the touch.

7. Place the pan on a cooling rack and cool completely while you make the frosting.

8. Turn the cake out onto a cutting board or work surface lined with parchment paper, with the bottom side of the cake facing up.

9. Cut the cake in half horizontally so that you have two pieces that are about 10 by 8 inches.

10. Spread the vanilla frosting across one of the halves, bottom side up.

11. Place the unfrosted half on top of the frosted half, making sure that the top side of the cake faces up and the bottom side of the cake faces the frosting.

12. In a double boiler, heat the chocolate chips until melted and smooth; spread the melted chocolate evenly over the top of the cake.

13. Place the cake in the refrigerator for 5 to 10 minutes to allow the chocolate to set up just a bit. Do not leave it in the refrigerator too long, or the chocolate will get too hard to cleanly cut.

14. Using a sharp knife, cut the cake into 10 smaller cakes that are about 2 by 4 inches each. To get clean cuts, wipe your knife clean with a towel each time you run it through the cake.

Chocolate Mocha Cake, page 32

Choco Raspberry Dream, page 38

Classic Vanilla Cake, page 49

Bunny Hugger's Carrot Cake, page 67

Cupcake Wars winning cupcakes, page 88

Piña Colada Cake, page 69

Little Devil, page 113

Sticky Buns, page 116

Love Bite

....

Canola Oil

"Canadian Oil, Low Acid" is what canola oil stands for. A product of Canada's rapeseed (which obviously needed a more delicate name, hence "canola"), this oil is tasty, smooth, buttery, and good for you. Even the FDA says so. Why? Because it's a simple little oil with very little saturation, meaning your body can easily move it around and break it down rather than it getting stuck in bendy little arteries. It's one of those "good-for-you" fats that help fat-soluble vitamins get to where they need to go in that body of yours. The omega-3s are known to help with heart health and reduce inflammation. But for the love of pie, do not heat canola oil over its smoke point, 400°F. Once you smoke oil, you degrade, oxidize, and partially hydrogenate it, which undoes all its good and turns it into a very, very bad oil.

Sticky Buns

Did you think we could start a bakery, take you back in time to the nostalgic deliciousness of sweet treats past, and not do a sticky cinnamon bun? That would be like Romeo without Juliet, New York without the City, rolling without the skates, summer without heat, rock without the roll, my glass without whiskey . . . it just wouldn't be right!

As far as ingredients go, this is a simple recipe. However, whenever you are baking bread, timing and technique are everything. In our store a sticky bun is made over the course of two days. We like to let the yeast work its magic, and the only way to do that is to give it time. One dough-rise at room temperature, another overnight in the fridge, then we roll it out, and, depending on how many people are waiting in line, the buns go into the proofer at a moist 90°F until they double in size or go back into the fridge to keep them from rising before we are ready. Bake until golden brown and not a shade darker. They will keep browning a bit once you take them out of the oven. It's a delicate dance indeed. But I have faith you can do it.

Do not, I repeat, *do not* eat the raw dough! Not because of the disease risks, but because your tummy is a warm, dark, moist place. Perfect for yeast growing and dough rising. Yes, it will rise in your belly and cause a bit of a disturbance.

If you are using a stand or hand mixer, use the dough hook attachment.

Makes 12 buns

FOR THE DOUGH

1 tablespoon active dry yeast

½ cup plus 2 tablespoons warm water

7 ½ cups plus 1 ½ tablespoons (2 pounds, 6 ounces) all-purpose flour

½ cup plus 1 ½ tablespoons (4.3 ounces) sugar

½ cup plus 2 tablespoons non-hydrogenated vegan margarine (recommended: Earth Balance)

1 teaspoon salt

2 ½ teaspoons egg replacer (recommended: Ener-G)

1 ¼ cups soymilk

FOR THE FILLING

½ cup non-hydrogenated vegan margarine (recommended: Earth Balance)

2 tablespoons sugar

1 tablespoon ground cinnamon

Optional Addition

1 cup chopped walnuts

FOR THE FROSTING

3 cups (13.5 ounces) powdered sugar

¼ to ½ cup water

1. Make the dough: In a large bowl, stir together the yeast, warm water, 1 ¼ cups of the flour, and 2 tablespoons of the sugar until combined. Let stand at room temperature to proof for 10 to 20 minutes, until it begins to bubble and rise to twice its size. You have just made the sponge.
2. Add the margarine, the remaining sugar, the salt, and egg replacer and mix to combine until only a few small lumps remain.
3. Add the soymilk and continue mixing.
4. Slowly add the remaining flour and mix until a solid dough mass forms; the dry ingredients should be incorporated and the dough should pull away from the sides of the bowl when mixing with a dough hook. If mixing by hand, the dough will be slightly sticky but not wet. This may take several minutes.

5. Cover the bowl of dough with a damp dish towel and set aside in a warm area of the room to proof until it doubles in size, about 1 hour.

6. Dust your table lightly with flour to prevent sticking. Remove the dough from the bowl and knead by hand for 1 to 2 minutes. Return it to the bowl, cover, and let it rest in the refrigerator overnight.

7. Make the filling: Mix the margarine, sugar, and cinnamon together in a bowl by hand or with a hand mixer. Cover and store in an airtight container in the refrigerator until ready to use.

8. Pull the dough from the refrigerator and turn it out onto a lightly floured work surface.

9. With a rolling pin, begin rolling the dough out until you have a rectangle that is 24 inches side to side and 12 inches top to bottom. If the dough springs back to a smaller size, let it rest for a few minutes so the gluten strands can relax, and try again.

10. Spread the filling evenly across the entire surface of the dough, leaving ½ to 1 inch at the top without filling. Sprinkle the walnuts over the filling, if using.

11. Starting at the bottom of the rectangle, begin to roll the dough in on itself until you get to the naked edge at the top.

12. Brush the edge with water and roll the dough across the wet edge to seal. Using a ruler to guide you, cut the dough into 2-inch rounds with a very sharp knife. You will end up with 12 rounds.

13. Line 2 baking sheets with parchment paper.

14. Place the rounds on the baking sheets, leaving about 4 inches between each bun so that you have 6 buns per sheet.

15. Loosely cover each tray of buns with a plastic bag or a moist towel and set aside in a warm area of the room to proof for about 1 hour, until the buns are triple their original size (see Note).

16. Meanwhile, preheat the oven to 350°F.

17. Remove the plastic from the sheets and place the sheets in the oven. Bake for 5 minutes.

18. Rotate the trays and bake for 5 more minutes, or until the buns are golden brown.
19. Make the frosting: Place the powdered sugar in a bowl and slowly stir in the water until a pourable consistency is reached.
20. Drizzle the frosting over the tops of the hot sticky buns. Enjoy while warm.

NOTE

Many factors play into the rise of the buns, so we cannot give a precise proofing time for this step. Room temperature, humidity, quality of yeast, and even how much you worked your dough all have an impact on how long your buns will need to sit before they are fully proofed. You can put the covered buns in a turned-off oven with a tray of hot water to create a steam proofer, which will help keep them warm and moist. Leave them there for 15 to 20 minutes, then remove them so you can preheat your oven. Be careful, though, because you can actually overproof your buns! If they begin to droop, flatten, or look melty, they are overproofing. You want them to be full, plump, and soft. (Insert "That's what *she* said" joke here.)

Chapter 5

Cookies

I am the only tough cookie in this kitchen. And that's how it's gonna stay.

Most cookie and cake recipes are very similar. The ingredients tend to be exactly the same but present in different amounts, such as less liquid and fat or a closer sugar-to-flour ratio. Make a few subtle changes to the mixing and the order of ingredients and ta-da, you have cookies.

Creaming the sugar is the foundation for cookie enjoyment. If you use dehydrated cane juice or turbinado sugar, the crystals will be a bit larger and stronger than standard white table sugar. Not creaming long enough can result in sandy, grainy cookies because the sugar crystals haven't been dissolved enough. No one likes a grainy cookie, so make sure the crystals are mostly broken down, and that the "cream" is good and airy before you add the other heavy and weighty ingredients. If you love the zing of the mixer, beware of overmixing and please proceed at slow speed. Stop often and scrape the sides of your bowl. This will ensure total incorporation but help avoid overmixing, Want a softer, chewier cookie? Dissolve half your sugar into the liquid ingredients. Or melt half of your margarine and add it in with the oil or liquid ingredients.

Cookie sandwiches, anyone?

This is a fun way to spruce up the average cookie, and another vehicle for frosting.

1. Choose your cookie. For softer sandwiches, reduce the baking time of your cookies by 1 minute.
2. Choose your frosting.
3. Choose your crunch: peanuts, chocolate chips, sprinkles, crushed candy, crispy rice . . .
4. Pipe or spread about 2 tablespoons of frosting on the bottom (flat) side of one cookie.
5. Place another cookie bottom side down on the frosted cookie.
6. Press together so the frosting reaches the edges.
7. Roll the sides of the cookies in the crunch of your choice.

New Chocolate Chip Cookies

This basic cookie recipe is our best-selling cookie to date. If you can master this recipe, the others will be easier than pie. But that is a whole other chapter, so let's focus on cookies first.

Makes 12 large or 24 small cookies

1 cup non-hydrogenated vegan
   margarine (recommended:
   Earth Balance)
1 cup plus 2 ½ tablespoons
   (8 ounces) sugar
1 cup plus 2 ½ tablespoons
   (8 ounces) lightly packed brown
   sugar
1 tablespoon vanilla extract

½ cup soymilk
½ cup vegetable or canola oil
4 cups (1 pound, 4 ounces)
   all-purpose flour
1 ½ teaspoons baking powder
1 ½ teaspoons baking soda
1 ½ teaspoons salt
1 cup chocolate chips

1. Preheat the oven to 350°F.
2. Line 2 baking sheets with parchment paper.
3. In the bowl of a stand mixer, combine the margarine, sugars, and vanilla and cream together with the paddle attachment until light and fluffy, 2 to 3 minutes. Scrape the bottom of the bowl and mix again to ensure all the ingredients are combined, about 30 seconds more.
4. In a separate bowl, whisk together the soymilk and oil. Slowly add the soymilk mixture to the sugar mixture and mix to combine.
5. In a separate bowl, whisk together the flour, baking powder, baking soda, and salt. Add to the sugar mixture and mix until a dough forms. Add the chocolate chips and stir to combine.
6. Scoop the dough onto the baking sheets with a spring-loaded ice cream scoop. Use a 2-ounce scoop for large cookies and a 1-ounce scoop for small.

Leave 2 to 3 inches between each cookie and gently pat them down with your fingertips.

7. Bake for 9 to 11 minutes, until the edges of the cookies begin to turn golden brown. Using a spatula, remove the cookies from the pan and set on a wire mesh rack to cool.

Love Bite

Milking the Bean

Imagine rows of happy bean pods soaking in the sun and rain. There they are singing along and happily producing milk that is good for you, better for the environment, and much easier on the cows. You don't need much of the soymama's milk, because every sip is filled with protein, healthy fats, and fiber. Getting milk from soybeans is much easier as well, as they don't run away when you try to milk them. Here at Sticky Fingers, the soymilk we use is both unflavored and unsweetened so we can be in charge of what is added. We are bossy and like to be in control of the sweet in our sweets.

Oatmeal Raisin Cookies

You never stop craving oatmeal raisin cookies, do you? Me neither, and I find them especially irresistible when they are oven-hot. I burn my tongue every time, and I'm proud of it.

Makes 12 large or 24 small cookies

1 cup non-hydrogenated vegan
  margarine (recommended:
  Earth Balance)
¾ cup plus 1 tablespoon
  (5.6 ounces) sugar
1 ½ cups (10.5 ounces) lightly
  packed brown sugar
1 teaspoon vanilla extract
½ cup soymilk
½ cup vegetable or canola oil

3 cups plus 3 tablespoons (1 pound)
  all-purpose flour
¾ cup plus 1 tablespoon (4 ounces)
  whole wheat pastry flour
2 teaspoons baking powder
2 teaspoons baking soda
1 teaspoon salt
2 cups (7 ounces) rolled oats
  (not instant)
¾ cup raisins

1. Preheat the oven to 350°F.
2. Line 2 baking sheets with parchment paper.
3. In the bowl of a stand mixer, combine the margarine, sugars, and vanilla and cream together with the paddle attachment until light and fluffy, 2 to 3 minutes.
4. In a separate bowl, whisk together the soymilk and oil. Slowly add the soymilk mixture to the sugar mixture and mix to combine.
5. In a separate bowl, combine the flours, baking powder, baking soda, and salt. Add the oats and raisins. Add the dry ingredients to the wet ingredients and mix until a dough forms.
6. Scoop the dough onto the baking sheets with a spring-loaded ice cream

scoop. Use a 2-ounce scoop for large cookies and a 1-ounce scoop for small. Leave 2 to 3 inches between each cookie and gently pat them down with your fingertips.

7. Bake for 9 to 11 minutes, until the edges of the cookies begin to brown. Using a spatula, remove the cookies from the pan and set on a wire mesh rack to cool.

Love Bite

I ♥ Oats

It's true! Oats have kept me hearty since I was young. Think of the oat as a chimney sweep for your arteries, a scrub brush for your veins, and a sponge for evil-doing LDL cholesterol. Seriously. The soluble fiber in oats has been proven to suck the LDL cholesterol right from your bloodstream, and the other healthy bits of antioxidants literally make your artery walls squeaky clean. So much so that cholesterol and plaque cannot build up, leaving your blood to run freely throughout your body. Quick feet, quick mind. They say at least a cup a day is best—how fortunate that these cookies are packed with the stuff. Seconds, anyone?

Lemon Coconut Cookies

If you love coconut, then this will be your favorite cookie ever. Coconut in and on the cookie will make you mad, but in a good way.

Makes 24 large or 36 small cookies

1 cup non-hydrogenated vegan
    margarine (recommended:
    Earth Balance)
1 ¾ cups plus ½ tablespoon
    (12.5 ounces) sugar
1 ½ cups (10.5 ounces) lightly
    packed brown sugar
1 teaspoon vanilla extract
⅛ teaspoon lemon oil, or more
    to taste
2 teaspoons lemon zest

2 ½ cups (6.8 ounces) shredded
    coconut, plus ¾ cup for topping
⅔ cup soymilk
¾ cup canola or vegetable oil
5 ¼ cups plus 2 ½ tablespoons
    (1 pound, 11 ounces)
    all-purpose flour
2 teaspoons baking powder
2 teaspoons baking soda
1 teaspoon salt

1. Preheat the oven to 350°F.
2. Line 2 baking sheets with parchment paper.
3. In the bowl of a stand mixer, combine the margarine, sugars, vanilla, lemon oil, and lemon zest and cream together with the paddle attachment until light and fluffy, 2 to 3 minutes.
4. Add the 2 ½ cups coconut and stir.
5. In a separate bowl, whisk together the soymilk and oil. Slowly add soymilk mixture to the sugar mixture and mix to combine.
6. In a separate bowl, combine the flour, baking powder, baking soda, and salt. Add the dry ingredients to the wet ingredients and mix until a dough forms.
7. Scoop the dough onto the baking sheets with a spring-loaded ice cream scoop. Use a 2-ounce scoop for large cookies and a 1-ounce scoop for small.

Leave 2 to 3 inches between each cookie and gently pat them down with your fingertips.

8. Sprinkle some of the remaining ¾ cup shredded coconut on top of each cookie.

9. Bake for 9 to 11 minutes, until the edges of the cookies begin to brown. Using a spatula remove the cookies from the pan and set on a wire mesh rack to cool.

Love Bite

Lemon Oil

Lemon oil packs an insane punch and gives fresh lemon flavor to everything you add it to. Throw out that artificial flavor—who needs it? Certainly not you, with this zesty new addition to your flavor arsenal. Don't fake it—lemon oil will make you forget there was ever another option.

Almond Linzer Cookies

This is a twist on one of the most famous cookies of all time. The almond and the raspberry are superb when enjoyed in the same mouthful. Anyone you share these with will fall in love with you, guaranteed.

Makes 12 large or 24 small cookies

1 cup plus ½ tablespoon
    (5.2 ounces) all-purpose flour
1 cup (4 ounces) almond flour
½ cup plus 1 tablespoon
    (2.4 ounces) powdered sugar,
    plus more for dusting
½ cup non-hydrogenated vegan
    margarine (recommended: Earth
    Balance), chilled and cut into
    ½-inch cubes

1 ½ teaspoons egg replacer
    (recommended: Ener-G)
2 tablespoons water
½ teaspoon almond extract
½ teaspoon vanilla extract
½ cup raspberry jam

1. In a large bowl, whisk together the all-purpose flour, almond flour, and powdered sugar. Using a fork or dough cutter, cut in the margarine and mix until small crumbs form.
2. In a small bowl, whisk together the egg replacer, water, and almond and vanilla extracts. Add the wet ingredients to the dry ingredients and mix until well combined. You can knead the dough with your hands at this point until everything comes together.
3. Wrap the dough in plastic wrap and refrigerate for at least 1 hour or overnight.
4. Preheat the oven to 350°F.
5. Line 2 baking sheets with parchment paper.
6. Lightly flour a clean work surface. Roll the dough out to ¼-inch thickness.

Cut out cookie shapes using a small or medium fluted round cutter or a heart-shaped cutter (whatever cute shape you have is fine).

7. Using a smaller version of your chosen cutter, cut holes in the center of half the cookies. (Half of the cookies will be solid, and half will have their centers cut out like a window.)

8. Place the cookies 1 inch apart on the baking sheets and bake for 5 to 6 minutes, until they appear dry. Be careful not to overbake!

9. Let cool in the pans for a few minutes, then transfer them to a cooling rack to cool completely.

10. Spoon raspberry jam on top of each solid cookie, using 1 teaspoon jam if making 24 cookies or 2 teaspoons jam if making 12 cookies. Place the "window" cookies on top.

11. Put some powdered sugar in a sifter and lightly dust the sandwiched cookies with the sugar.

Love Bite

Almonds

California is often the place where health crazes and fitness frenzies are born. So it's no surprise that it's where almonds are grown. They are not only delicious; these little bits of perfection can keep you healthy as well, giving you more reason to add them to any meal, including dessert. Containing alpha-tocopherol, your body's number-one favorite form of vitamin E, this nutty nutrient helps fight off free radicals, helps keep cholesterol levels low, and generally keeps you healthy and young. Some even theorize that the healthy bacteria in your body might benefit from the almonds you eat.

Pecan Cookies

The buttery flavor of this pecan cookie is outstanding. The smell alone is going to bring you to your knees.

Makes 12 large or 24 small cookies

¾ cup non-hydrogenated vegan margarine (recommended: Earth Balance)

1 cup plus 2 tablespoons (8 ounces) sugar

1 ¾ cups plus 1 ½ tablespoons (13 ounces) lightly packed brown sugar

2 teaspoons vanilla extract

¾ cup soymilk

⅔ cup vegetable or canola oil

4 ¾ cups plus 1 tablespoon (1 pound, 8 ounces) all-purpose flour

2 teaspoons baking powder

2 teaspoons baking soda

1 ½ teaspoons salt

1 ½ cup pecans, halves and pieces

1. Preheat the oven to 350°F.
2. Line 2 baking sheets with parchment paper.
3. In the bowl of a stand mixer, combine the margarine, sugars, and vanilla and cream together with the paddle attachment until light and fluffy, 2 to 3 minutes. Scrape the bottom of the bowl and mix again to ensure that all the ingredients are combined, about 30 seconds more.
4. In a separate bowl, whisk together the soymilk and oil. Slowly add the soymilk mixture to the sugar mixture and mix to combine.
5. In a separate bowl, combine the flour, baking powder, baking soda and salt. Add the pecans. Add the dry ingredients to the wet ingredients and mix until a dough forms.

6. Scoop the dough onto the baking sheets with a spring-loaded ice cream scoop. Use a 2-ounce scoop for large cookies and a 1-ounce scoop for small. Leave 2 to 3 inches between each cookie and gently pat them down with your fingertips.

7. Bake for 9 to 11 minutes, until the edges of the cookies begin to brown.

8. Using a spatula, remove the cookies from the pan and set on a wire mesh rack to cool.

Peanut Butter Cookies

Remember when you discovered how to make the fork marks in your peanut butter cookies? I recall the day when Mom and I were making cookies together and she revealed the secret of the fork marks to me. I looked up at her and saw a bright white light surrounding her being; she placed the fork into my hand and told me to go forth and share the fork-marked peanut butter cookies with the masses.

Makes 12 large and 24 small

1 ¼ cups non-hydrogenated vegan margarine (recommended: Earth Balance)

3 cups peanut butter

1 cup plus 3 tablespoons (8.5 ounces) sugar

1 cup plus 3 tablespoons (8.5 ounces) lightly packed brown sugar

2 teaspoons vanilla extract

¼ cup water

¼ cup soymilk

3 ⅓ cups (1 pound, 0.5 ounce) all-purpose flour

2 teaspoons baking soda

2 teaspoons baking powder

¼ teaspoon salt

⅓ cup chopped peanuts (optional)

1. Preheat the oven to 350°F.
2. Line 2 baking sheets with parchment paper.
3. In the bowl of a stand mixer, combine the margarine, peanut butter, sugars, and vanilla and cream together with the paddle attachment until light and fluffy, 2 to 3 minutes.
4. In a separate bowl, whisk together the water and soymilk. Slowly add the soymilk mixture to the peanut butter mixture and mix to combine.
5. In another separate bowl, whisk together the flour, baking soda, baking powder, and salt. Add the peanuts, if using.
6. Add the dry ingredients to the wet ingredients and mix until a dough forms.
7. Scoop the dough onto the baking sheets with a spring-loaded ice cream

scoop. Use a 2-ounce scoop for large cookies and a 1-ounce scoop for small. Leave 2 to 3 inches between each cookie.

8. Make a crisscross pattern on top of each cookie with a fork.

9. Bake for 9 to 11 minutes, until the edges of the cookies begin to brown.

10. Using a spatula, remove the cookies from the pan and set on a wire mesh rack to cool.

Love Bite

Peanuts

Peanuts are rich in antioxidants and minerals and carry a whopping 9 grams of protein per 1/4 cup serving. It is true that those with an allergy to this legume can have extreme and life-threatening reactions, but rest assured that it's a small percentage of the population and you can easily be tested to find out if you are in the no-peanut category. It is proper allergy etiquette to check with party throwers before showing up with a triple batch of peanut butter cookies.

Sweet-n-Salty Cookies

Chocolate and salt? You true foodies have never balked at the uncommon combo, have you? New to salty chocolate? Try any of those fancy salts; the precious pink fleur de sel, or the smoky, dark black salt. Be sure someone is there to catch you as you take your first bite, as you just might fall over.

Makes 12 large and 24 small cookies

¾ cup non-hydrogenated vegan margarine (recommended: Earth Balance)

1 cup plus 2 tablespoons (8 ounces) sugar

1 cup (7 ounces) lightly packed brown sugar

1 teaspoon vanilla extract

½ cup soymilk

½ cup vegetable or canola oil

3 ½ cups plus 1 ½ tablespoons (1 pound, 2 ounces) all-purpose flour

2 teaspoons baking powder

2 teaspoons baking soda

1 teaspoon salt

1 ¼ cups (4.4 ounces) rolled oats (not instant)

1 ¼ cups chocolate chips

2 tablespoons fleur de sel or gourmet salt of your choosing

1. Preheat the oven to 350°F.
2. Line 2 baking sheets with parchment paper.
3. In the bowl of a stand mixer, combine the margarine, sugars, and vanilla and cream together with the paddle attachment until light and fluffy, 2 to 3 minutes. Scrape the bottom of the bowl and mix again to ensure that all the ingredients are combined, about 30 seconds more.
4. In a separate bowl, whisk together the soymilk and oil. Slowly add the soymilk mixture to the sugar mixture and mix to combine.
5. In another separate bowl, combine the flour, baking powder, baking soda,

and salt. Add the oats and chocolate chips. Add the dry ingredients to the wet ingredients and mix until a dough forms.

6. Scoop the dough onto the baking sheets with a spring-loaded ice cream scoop. Use a 2-ounce scoop for large cookies and a 1-ounce scoop for small. Leave 2 to 3 inches between each cookie and gently pat them down with your fingertips.

7. Bake for 9 to 11 minutes, until the edges of the cookies begin to brown.

8. Remove from the oven and immediately sprinkle the tops of each cookie with fleur de sel (about ⅛ teaspoon over each one). Using a spatula, remove the cookies from the pan and set on a wire mesh rack to cool.

Double Chocolate Cookies

Cocoa and dark chocolate, reunited and revisited in cookie form. Go soft for cookie sandwiches, or go crunchy 'cause you want to. Either way, you are sure to covet them.

Makes 24 cookies

¾ cup non-hydrogenated vegan margarine (recommended: Earth Balance)

1 cup plus 2 tablespoons (8 ounces) sugar

1 cup (7 ounces) lightly packed brown sugar

½ teaspoon vanilla extract

½ cup soymilk

½ cup vegetable or canola oil

3 cups (15 ounces) all-purpose flour

1 cup (4 ounces) cocoa powder

½ teaspoon baking powder

1 ½ teaspoons baking soda

½ teaspoon salt

½ cup dark chocolate chips or pistoles

1. In the bowl of a stand mixer, combine the margarine, sugars, and vanilla and cream together with a paddle attachment until fluffy, 2 to 3 minutes. Scrape the bottom of the bowl and mix again to ensure that all the ingredients are combined, about 30 seconds more.

2. In a separate bowl, whisk together the soymilk and oil. Slowly add the soymilk mixture to the sugar mixture and mix to combine.

3. In another separate bowl, whisk together the all-purpose flour, cocoa powder, baking powder, baking soda, and salt. Add to the wet ingredients and mix until combined.

4. Scrape the dough from the bowl onto a clean work surface. Roll the dough into a 12-inch log. Cover with plastic wrap and refrigerate for a minimum of 2 hours.

5. Preheat the oven to 350°F.

6. Line 2 baking sheets with parchment paper.

7. Remove the dough from the refrigerator and slice into ½-inch-thick rounds. (If the dough begins to get too warm, it may become crumbly and difficult to work with. If this happens, return the dough to the refrigerator between batches to keep it firm.)

8. Place the rounds on the baking sheet 2 to 3 inches apart. Press a few chocolate chips or one pistole in the center of each cookie. Bake for 9 to 11 minutes, until the tops look crackly and dry.

9. Using a spatula, remove the cookies from the pans and set on a wire mesh rack to cool.

Phat Mint

These cookies are so minty cool, they are super phat, super dope, and delicious. You will be psyched when you get them out of the oven.

Makes 12 large and 24 small cookies

½ cup non-hydrogenated vegan margarine (recommended: Earth Balance)

¾ cup (5.5 ounces) sugar

⅔ cup plus ½ tablespoon (4.9 ounces) lightly packed brown sugar

1 teaspoon peppermint extract

¼ cup soymilk

⅓ cup vegetable or canola oil

2 cups (10 ounces) all-purpose flour

½ cup (2 ounces) cocoa powder

1 teaspoon baking powder

1 teaspoon baking soda

½ teaspoon salt

1. Preheat the oven to 350°F.
2. Line 2 baking sheets with parchment paper.
3. In the bowl of a stand mixer, combine the margarine, sugars, and peppermint extract and cream together with the paddle attachment until light and fluffy, 2 to 3 minutes.
4. In a separate bowl, whisk together the soymilk and oil. Slowly add the soymilk mixture to the sugar mixture and stir to combine.
5. In another separate bowl, combine the flour, cocoa powder, baking powder, baking soda, and salt. Add the dry ingredients to the wet ingredients and mix until a dough forms.
6. Scoop the dough onto the baking sheets with a spring-loaded ice cream scoop. Use a 2-ounce scoop for large cookies and a 1-ounce scoop for small. Leave 2 to 3 inches between each cookie and gently pat them down with your fingertips.
7. Bake for 11 to 15 minutes, until the tops of the cookies begin to crack.
8. Using a spatula, remove the cookies from the pan and set on a wire mesh rack to cool.

Sugar Cookies

Have your cookie cutters been sitting around, collecting dust, not living up to their potential? Look no further; this is the recipe for you and your favorite shaped sweets. Don't forget the decor (drizzle frosting, sprinkles, silver pearls) so your cookies will be dazzling and delicious.

Makes 24 to 36 cookies

1 cup non-hydrogenated vegan margarine (recommended: Earth Balance)

1 1/2 cups (10.5 ounces) sugar

1 to 2 drops lemon oil, to taste (optional)

2/3 cup soymilk

2 teaspoons lemon juice

2 teaspoons vanilla extract

4 cups plus 2 1/2 tablespoons (1 pound, 4.8 ounces) all-purpose flour

1 tablespoon baking powder

1/2 teaspoon salt

1. In the bowl of a stand mixer, combine the margarine, sugar, and lemon oil, if using, and cream together with the paddle attachment until light and fluffy, 2 to 3 minutes.
2. Slowly add the soymilk, lemon juice, and vanilla to the sugar mixture and mix to combine.
3. In a separate bowl, whisk together the flour, baking powder, and salt.
4. Add the dry ingredients to the wet ingredients and mix until a dough forms.
5. Wrap the dough in plastic wrap and refrigerate for at least 2 hours.
6. Preheat the oven to 350°F.
7. Line 2 baking sheets with parchment paper.
8. Remove the dough from the refrigerator. Place the dough between 2 sheets of parchment and roll out to 1/4-inch thickness.

9. Cut with cookie cutters in the shape of your choice and place on the parchment-lined baking sheets. If the dough becomes too soft to work with, return it to the refrigerator to firm up.

10. Bake for 7 to 10 minutes, until the edges of the cookies just begin to lightly brown.

11. Using a spatula, remove the cookies from the pan and set on a wire mesh rack to cool.

Gingerbread Cookies

Gingerbread is known for its structural capabilities in house building and people making, but we feel that these gingerbread cookies should be in the cookie mix all year long; their taste is simply too alluring to be confined to one season. Fill the cookie jar in March, serve with your favorite sorbet in June, and continue to devour in December.

Makes 24 to 30 cookies

2/3 cup non-hydrogenated vegan margarine (recommended: Earth Balance)

2/3 cup plus 1/2 tablespoon (5 ounces) lightly packed brown sugar

1 tablespoon egg replacer (recommended: Ener-G)

1 tablespoon water

1 tablespoon canola oil

1/3 cup molasses

2 1/4 cups plus 2 1/2 tablespoons (12 ounces) whole wheat pastry flour

1 teaspoon baking soda

1 1/2 teaspoons ground ginger

3/4 teaspoon ground cinnamon

1/4 teaspoon ground cloves

1/2 teaspoon salt

1. In the bowl of a stand mixer, combine the margarine and brown sugar and cream together with the paddle attachment until light and fluffy, 2 to 3 minutes. Scrape the bottom of the bowl and mix again to ensure that the ingredients are incorporated.
2. In a separate bowl, mix together the egg replacer and water.
3. Add the egg replacer mixture, oil, and molasses to the sugar mixture and stir to combine.
4. In a separate bowl, whisk together the flour, baking soda, ginger, cinnamon, cloves, and salt. Add the dry ingredients to the wet ingredients and mix until a dough forms.

5. Wrap the dough in plastic wrap and refrigerate for at least 2 hours.

6. Preheat the oven to 350°F.

7. Line 2 baking sheets with parchment paper.

8. Remove the dough from the refrigerator. Place the dough between 2 sheets of parchment paper and roll out to ¼-inch thickness.

9. Cut with cookie cutters in the shape of your choice and place on the parchment-lined baking sheets. If the dough becomes too soft to work with, return it to the refrigerator between batches to firm up.

10. Bake for 10 to 12 minutes, until the edges of the cookies begin to brown.

11. Using a spatula, remove the cookies from the pan and set on a wire mesh rack to cool.

Love Bite

Molasses

Molasses is the by-product moles make when they burrow into the ground. Just kidding. But I heard you giggle. Seriously, molasses has some great qualities, and blackstrap is the best variety, as this sweet syrup contains iron, calcium, and lots of other minerals. These nutrients are carried on a stream of brown sugar, which, according to some sources, makes them more easily absorbed and utilized. And there is nothing better than a stream of brown sugar.

Biscotti

The busiest and bossiest cookie recipe around. Not for the faint of heart or those with a short attention span. These cookies take time and patience, but they are worth the wait! They are great for dunking, coating, or just plain eating. Keep in a sealed glass jar for longer keeping and place where they can be seen so visitors know what an ace baker you are! And remember—any of these recipes can be made in a chocolate-dipped version (see page 148).

Chocolate Biscotti

An alternative mission statement for Sticky Fingers: "Adding more chocolate to any edible we can get our hands on."

Makes 12 biscotti

½ cup non-hydrogenated vegan margarine (recommended: Earth Balance)

½ cup plus 1 tablespoon (4 ounces) sugar

1 ½ teaspoons vanilla extract

1 ½ tablespoons water

1 teaspoon egg replacer (recommended: Ener-G)

⅔ cup soymilk

2 cups (10 ounces) all-purpose flour

⅔ cup (3.4 ounces) whole wheat pastry flour

½ cup (2 ounces) cocoa powder

1 teaspoon baking powder

1 teaspoon salt

½ cup chocolate chips

1. Preheat the oven to 350°F.
2. Line a baking sheet with parchment paper.
3. In the bowl of a stand mixer, combine the margarine, sugar, and vanilla and cream together with the paddle attachment until light and fluffy, about 3 minutes. Scrape the sides and bottom of the bowl and mix on high speed about 1 more minute.
4. In a small bowl, whisk together the water and egg replacer. Add the egg replacer mixture to the sugar mixture and stir to combine.
5. Add the soymilk and stir until all the ingredients are incorporated.
6. In a separate bowl, whisk together the flours, cocoa powder, baking powder, and salt. Add the chocolate chips. Slowly add the dry ingredients to the wet ingredients and mix until combined.
7. Scoop the dough out onto a clean work surface and press it into a 9 by 6-inch log; place the log on the baking sheet. Bake for 15 minutes.

8. Remove from the oven and let cool until cool enough that it can be worked with.

9. Cut the log into ¾ by 6-inch pieces and lay the pieces on their sides. Bake again for 15 to 20 minutes, until the pieces are dry. Leave on the pan and set it on a wire mesh rack to cool.

Love Bite

Whole Wheat Pastry Flour

Whole wheat pastry flour is a blessing in disguise. This inconspicuous light brown flour is capable of much more than simple recipes. Pastry flour is higher in gluten, the protein in wheat that holds baked goods together so tastefully. The whole wheat version has the healthy grain intact, making it a great source of protein, B vitamins, and fiber. And here is the best part—you can't taste how healthy it is, I swear.

Almond Biscotti

Almond has such a warm and comforting flavor that this cookie practically hugs you while you devour it.

Makes 12 biscotti

½ cup non-hydrogenated vegan margarine (recommended: Earth Balance)

½ cup plus 1 tablespoon (4 ounces) sugar

1 teaspoon almond extract

½ teaspoon vanilla extract

1 ½ tablespoons water

1 teaspoon egg replacer (recommended: Ener-G)

⅔ cup soymilk

2 ¼ cups plus 2 ½ tablespoons (12 ounces) all-purpose flour

⅔ cup (3.4 ounces) whole wheat pastry flour

1 teaspoon baking powder

1 teaspoon salt

⅓ cup toasted almond slices (see Note, page 61)

1. Preheat the oven to 350°F.
2. Line a baking sheet with parchment paper.
3. In the bowl of a stand mixer, combine the margarine, sugar, and almond and vanilla extracts and cream together with the paddle attachment until light and fluffy, about 3 minutes. Scrape the sides and bottom of the bowl and mix on high speed about 1 more minute.
4. In a small bowl, whisk together the water and egg replacer. Add the egg replacer mixture to the sugar mixture and stir to combine.
5. Add the soymilk and stir until all the ingredients are incorporated.
6. In a separate bowl, whisk together the flours, baking powder, and salt. Add the almonds. Slowly add the dry ingredients to the wet ingredients and mix until combined.

7. Scoop the dough out onto a clean work surface and press it into a 9 by 6-inch log; place the log on the baking sheet. Bake for 15 minutes.

8. Remove from the oven and let cool until it is cool enough that it can be worked with.

9. Cut the log into ¾ by 6-inch pieces and lay the pieces on their sides. Bake again for 15 to 20 minutes, until the pieces are dry.

10. Leave in the pan and set it on a wire mesh rack to cool.

VARIATION: CHOCOLATE-DIPPED BISCOTTI

Melt ½ cup chocolate chips in a double boiler over low heat until smooth, or microwave until melted. Add 1 tablespoon canola oil to thin the chocolate out. Dunk the ends of your biscotti into the chocolate and lay on parchment or waxed paper to set.

Hazelnut Biscotti

azelnuts are the cutest of nuts by far. I love these little guys! But don't be fooled, we have a nut with a serious Napoleon complex here—they nearly jump out of their skins and punch you in the face with their distinctive flavor. Look out!

Makes 12 biscotti

½ cup non-hydrogenated vegan margarine (recommended: Earth Balance)

½ cup plus 1 tablespoon (4 ounces) sugar

1 teaspoon hazelnut extract

½ teaspoon vanilla extract

1 ½ tablespoons water

1 teaspoon egg replacer (recommended: Ener-G)

⅔ cup soymilk

2 ¼ cups plus 2 ½ tablespoons (12 ounces) all-purpose flour

⅔ cup (3.4 ounces) whole wheat pastry flour

1 teaspoon baking powder

1 teaspoon salt

⅓ cup chopped toasted hazelnuts (see Note, page 59)

1. Preheat the oven to 350°F.
2. Line a baking sheet with parchment paper.
3. In the bowl of a stand mixer, combine the margarine, sugar, and hazelnut and vanilla extracts with the paddle attachment until light and fluffy, about 3 minutes. Scrape the sides and bottom of the bowl and mix on high speed about 1 more minute.
4. In a small bowl, whisk together the water and egg replacer. Add the egg replacer mixture to the sugar mixture and stir to combine.
5. Add the soymilk and stir until all the ingredients are incorporated.
6. In a separate bowl, whisk together the flours, baking powder, and salt. Add the hazelnuts. Slowly add the dry ingredients to the wet ingredients and mix until combined.

7. Scoop the dough out onto a clean work surface and press it into a 9 by 6-inch log; place the log on the baking sheet. Bake for 15 minutes.

8. Remove from the oven and let cool until it is cool enough that it can be worked with.

9. Cut the log into ¾ by 6-inch pieces and lay the pieces on their sides. Bake again for 15 to 20 minutes, until the pieces are dry.

10. Leave in the pan and set it on a wire mesh rack to cool.

Love Bite

Hazelnuts

Here is another superfood to chew on, another ingredient that just may save your life! It's so good for your heart I think it's even CPR certified. With antioxidants twenty times stronger than vitamin C, you no longer have any reason not to enjoy its flavorful benefits. Flavor is where it's at, as the flavones are where the benefits reside, and these compounds contain the antioxidant qualities that keep you healthy and strong.

Anisette Biscotti

My Grandpa Cellura never ate a cookie he couldn't dunk. Utilitarian at heart, he wanted to be able to drink his coffee and eat his cookie at the same time so he could hurry up and get back to fidgeting with things. God bless him. Here is a Grandpa Cellura–approved dunkin' cookie that will hold up to any coffee situation and please even the most fidgety grandpa.

Makes 12 biscotti

½ cup non-hydrogenated vegan margarine (recommended: Earth Balance)

½ cup plus 1 tablespoon (4 ounces) sugar

1 teaspoon anise extract or 2 tablespoons anisette liqueur

½ teaspoon vanilla extract

1 ½ tablespoons water

1 teaspoon egg replacer (recommended: Ener-G)

2/3 cup soymilk

2 ¼ cups plus 2 ½ tablespoons (12 ounces) all-purpose flour

¾ cup (3.4 ounces) whole wheat pastry flour

1 teaspoon baking powder

1 teaspoon salt

2 teaspoons ground aniseed

1. Preheat the oven to 350°F.
2. Line a baking sheet with parchment paper.
3. In the bowl of a stand mixer, combine the margarine, sugar, and anise and vanilla extracts and cream together with the paddle attachment until light and fluffy, about 3 minutes. Scrape the sides and bottom of the bowl and mix on high speed about 1 more minute.
4. In a small bowl, whisk together the water and egg replacer. Add the egg replacer mixture to the sugar mixture and stir to combine.
5. Add the soymilk and stir until all the ingredients are incorporated.

6. In a separate bowl, whisk together the flours, baking powder, salt, and aniseed. Slowly add the dry ingredients to the wet ingredients and mix until combined.

7. Scoop the dough out onto a clean work surface and press it into a 9 by 6-inch log; place the log on the baking sheet. Bake for 15 minutes.

8. Remove from the oven and let cool until it is cool enough that it can be worked with.

9. Cut the log into ¾ by 6-inch pieces and lay the pieces on their sides. Bake again for 15 to 20 minutes, until the pieces are dry.

10. Leave in the pan and set it on a wire mesh rack to cool.

Love Bite

Anisette

Not only my favorite song by June of 44, anisette is also an aroma I grew up with. Anisette, fennel seed, and licorice were my grandmother's favorite flavors. They went with everything Sicilian, and she put them in everything: cannoli, meatballs, arancini, stew, brownies, you name it. This isn't as much of a Love Bite as it is walk down memory lane with mad props to Gram and Gramps. Big love for feeding me all of the amazing flavors that keep me craving, creating, and baking.

Chapter 6

Muffins, Breads, and Scones

The cake you can eat for breakfast.

Muffins, breads, and scones are sweet and satisfying ways to start your day, and you shouldn't be ashamed. The redeeming qualities of muffins are plentiful, so don't worry one bit. But before you can break your fast with one of these mouth pleasers, there are some rules you need to know.

There is technique to making the perfect muffin top: You need to slightly undermix or you risk the forbidden and frowned-upon volcano top, or the ever-so-ugly flat top. It's similar to the rules you use when choosing the proper pants—too tight and our muffin top explodes, too loose and our curves look flat. We want that perfect curve and slight lip on the side, and just the right amount of crunch on the top. How, you may ask? The method is all in the mix. You want to stir enough to moisten the batter, and lumps are imperative. Alert! You only need to mix fifteen to thirty strokes once all the ingredients are in the bowl, making muffins easy to mix by hand. This is more difficult with a hand or stand mixer, but attainable: Put the mixer on low speed and scrape the sides of the bowl only once or twice. That crunchy top is simply a bit of the sugar crystallizing while in the oven. And as we all know, crunch is always a complement to soft treats, so we like to turn it up. You can sprinkle toppings such as nuts and oats, or a light dusting of brown sugar and spice right before your muffins go in the oven if you want to up the ante.

Blueberry Muffins

Blueberries are spectacular. Their antioxidant and anti-inflammatory effects are unmatched by any other berry. And the blues, reds, and greens that make the blueberry so breathtaking are also the place where the nutrients lie.

Makes 12 muffins

FOR THE MUFFINS

2 tablespoons non-hydrogenated vegan margarine (recommended: Earth Balance)

2/3 cup (4.4 ounces) sugar

1/4 cup (1.7 ounces) lightly packed brown sugar

1/2 cup soymilk

1/4 cup vegetable or canola oil

1 1/2 teaspoons lemon juice

1 teaspoon vanilla extract

1 1/2 teaspoons egg replacer (recommended: Ener-G)

1/3 cup water

1 1/4 cups (6.3 ounces) all-purpose flour

1 cup (5 ounces) whole wheat pastry flour

1 teaspoon baking powder

1/4 teaspoon baking soda

1/4 teaspoon salt

1 cup blueberries

FOR THE OAT TOPPING

1/4 cup rolled oats (not instant)

2 tablespoons evaporated cane sugar

2 tablespoons brown sugar

1. Preheat the oven to 350°F.
2. Line a standard muffin tin with 12 paper liners.
3. Make the muffins: In the bowl of a stand mixer, combine the margarine and sugars, and cream together with the paddle attachment.

4. In a small bowl, whisk together the soymilk, oil, lemon juice, and vanilla. Add to the sugar mixture and mix until combined.

5. In another small bowl, whisk together the egg replacer and water. Add to the sugar mixture and mix until combined.

6. In a large bowl, combine the flours, baking powder, baking soda, and salt. Add to the wet ingredients and stir until just mixed. Do not overmix the batter.

7. Fold in the blueberries by hand.

8. Make the oat topping: In a small bowl, stir all the topping ingredients together.

9. Fill the muffin cups two-thirds full and sprinkle 1 to 2 teaspoons of the oat topping on top of each muffin.

10. Bake for 20 minutes, or until a toothpick inserted in the center of a muffin comes out clean. Leave in the pan and set on a wire mesh rack to cool.

Love Bite

....

Protein

We could talk about protein for hours. What isn't it good for? What doesn't it do? I'm pretty sure you all know its main functions, like building muscle, forming energy, and such. One thing that stands out in my years of learning about and loving protein is the way the body can reuse amino acids to make protein. Whether it's the amino acids from the enzymes in your saliva, the amino acids from muscular breakdown after an intense workout, or the amino acids from the gluten and soy protein in your breakfast muffin, these amino acids enter your bloodstream and end up in a "pool" of useable amino acids or are broken down into carbohydrates. Amino acids are simply carbohydrates with an amino group attached, FYI. If there is an overabundance of one type of amino but less of another in the pool, carbohydrates can swap those amino groups, attempting to balance the essential amino acids you need.

Back to that intense workout: Those loads of lunges you just did actually broke down the muscle just a tiny bit. Now it wants to rebuild, so it sends out a request of sorts for some protein building. Messenger proteins start pulling from the pool of available amino acids to rebuild or synthesize. If any essential aminos are missing, the chain will fall apart and the aminos, if in good shape, will return to the pool, available for later use. This is why eating after a workout helps with recovery. If you don't have all the aminos you need, you'll just end up sore and tired after your workout. No fun. But you never know, the aminos in your saliva could one day help save your biceps, or the protein in your morning breakfast muffin might make the enzymes that keep you moving. Incredible.

Banana Chimp Muffins

These muffins are so delish, they are sure to win over the cheekiest of monkeys!

Makes 12 muffins

¼ cup non-hydrogenated vegan margarine (recommended: Earth Balance)

½ cup plus 1 tablespoon (4 ounces) sugar

½ teaspoon vanilla extract

6 ounces ripe bananas (about 3 bananas, peeled)

½ cup soymilk

2 cups plus 1 tablespoon (10.25 ounces) all-purpose flour

1 ½ teaspoons baking powder

½ teaspoon baking soda

¼ teaspoon salt

½ cup chocolate chips

1. Preheat the oven to 350°F.
2. Line a standard muffin tin with 12 paper liners.
3. In the bowl of a stand mixer, combine the margarine, sugar, and vanilla and cream together with the paddle attachment.
4. Add the bananas and mix until the bananas are nice and mashed.
5. Slowly add the soymilk and mix until completely incorporated.
6. In a separate bowl, combine the flour, baking powder, baking soda, and salt. Add the dry ingredients to the wet ingredients and mix until just incorporated. Stir in the chocolate chips.
7. Fill the muffin cups two-thirds full and bake for 25 to 30 minutes, until a toothpick inserted into a muffin comes out clean. Leave on the pan and set it on a wire mesh rack to cool.

VARIATION: BANANA CHIMP LOAF

Make the batter as above. Lightly grease and flour a loaf (9 by 5-inch, or 1-pound) pan. Pour your prepared batter in and bake for 45 minutes to 1 hour, until a toothpick inserted in the center comes out clean. If the top of your loaf starts to get too dark before the center is done, cover the pan with foil. Leave in the pan and set it on a wire mesh rack to cool.

Love Bite

Vitamin B

Whenever the subject of veganism comes up, inevitably there's a discussion about vitamin B_{12}. For now it's time to talk about another vitamin in the family, vitamin B_6. Equally as crucial to your life, vitamin B_6 is a coenzyme of numerous enzymes that are involved in all amino acid metabolism, as well as in the metabolism of neurotransmitters of glycogen, heme iron, important hormones, and a few other major processes needed for existence. What does this mean? It means that any time your body makes or uses an amino acid, vitamin B_6 is involved, and that includes just about everything. Vegetarian sources like bananas and oats are two good choices to get you dosed up on this lifesaver.

Banana Walnut Muffins

One more way to get your delicious daily dose of potassium and omega-3s.

Makes 12 muffins

¼ cup non-hydrogenated vegan margarine (recommended: Earth Balance)

½ cup plus 1 tablespoon (4 ounces) sugar

½ teaspoon vanilla extract

6 ounces ripe bananas (about 3 bananas, peeled)

½ cup soymilk

2 cups plus 1 tablespoon (10.25 ounces) all-purpose flour

1 ½ teaspoons baking powder

½ teaspoon baking soda

¼ teaspoon salt

½ cup chopped walnuts

1. Preheat the oven to 350°F.
2. Line a standard muffin tin with 12 paper liners.
3. In the bowl of a stand mixer, combine the margarine, sugar, and vanilla and cream together with the paddle attachment.
4. Add the bananas and mix until they are nice and mashed.
5. Slowly add the soymilk and mix until completely incorporated.
6. In a separate bowl, combine the flour, baking powder, baking soda, and salt. Add the dry ingredients to the wet ingredients and mix until just incorporated. Stir in the walnuts.
7. Fill the muffin cups two-thirds full and bake for 25 to 30 minutes, until a toothpick inserted into a muffin comes out clean. Leave in the pan and set on a wire mesh rack to cool.

VARIATION: BANANA WALNUT LOAF

Make the batter as above. Lightly grease and flour a loaf (9 by 5-inch, or 1-pound) pan. Pour the batter in and bake for 45 minutes to 1 hour, until a toothpick inserted in the center comes out clean. If the top of your loaf starts to get too dark before the center is done, cover the pan with foil. Leave in the pan and set on a wire mesh rack to cool.

Love Bite

Carbohydrates

"Carbohydrate" (whisper) has almost become a dirty word. Carbohydrates have been ostracized, removed from menus, blamed for fatigue, and made to feel inadequate and responsible for belly fat everywhere. Well, my friends, I'm here to help clean up the carbo image. Carbohydrates are one of our most necessary nutrients, and the one you need in the largest quantity. Water, fat, protein, and carbs are the macro ingredients that keep you alive, and so necessary is the carb that without this one nutrient, your body will literally break itself down, turning muscle and fat into glycogen, the usable form of carbohydrate in your body. Morphing from one nutrient into another to save a life? That's some serious superhero powers! Enough with the slams, the bad-mouthing, the banning, and the bashing. Celebrate, load up, and liberate! Shout with me: "I LOVE CARBS!!!"

Lemon Poppy Seed Muffins

Good thing poppies are known for having an antispasmodic effect. You will be calmed to a lull after completely spazzing out from sinking your teeth into one of these. But unless you want to be in a food coma for the rest of the day, don't eat the entire batch in one sitting, please and thank you.

Makes 12 muffins

FOR THE MUFFINS

2 tablespoons non-hydrogenated vegan margarine (recommended: Earth Balance)

½ cup plus 1 ½ tablespoons (4.2 ounces) sugar

2 tablespoons brown sugar

½ cup soymilk

⅓ cup vegetable or canola oil

3 tablespoons lemon juice

1 teaspoon vanilla extract

1 to 2 drops lemon oil, to taste

1 ½ teaspoons egg replacer (recommended: Ener-G)

¼ cup water

2 cups plus 3 tablespoons (11 ounces) all-purpose flour

1 teaspoon baking powder

½ teaspoon baking soda

½ teaspoon salt

2 tablespoons poppy seeds

FOR THE LEMON GLAZE

1 cup powdered sugar

2 to 3 tablespoons lemon juice

made cake mm good!!

1. Preheat the oven to 350°F.
2. Line a standard muffin tin with 12 paper liners.
3. In the bowl of a stand mixer, combine the margarine and sugars, and cream together with the paddle attachment.
4. In a small bowl, whisk together the soymilk, oil, lemon juice, vanilla, and lemon oil. Add to the sugar mixture and mix until combined.

5. In another small bowl, whisk together the egg replacer and water. Add to the sugar mixture and mix until combined.

6. In a large bowl, combine the flour, baking powder, baking soda, salt, and poppy seeds. Add to the wet ingredients and stir until just mixed. Do not overmix the batter.

7. Fill the muffin cups two-thirds full. Bake for 25 to 30 minutes, until a toothpick inserted in the center of a muffin comes out clean. Leave in the pan and set it on a wire mesh rack to cool.

8. Make the glaze: Place the powdered sugar in a small bowl. Slowly add enough lemon juice to reach the desired consistency. Once cooled, remove the muffins from the pan and drizzle the tops with glaze.

Love Bite

Energy

We know the energy basics, right? Everything has energy of some sort, whether it's potential (stored) or kinetic (motion). And, as you can imagine, the food you eat produces energy, comes from energy, and contains energy. But foods also have the energy known as gravitational pull. You will see it happen, for sure. These treats actually pull people's mouths directly toward the treat's location. As you begin trying and testing, friends you haven't seen for years will be stopping by. The FedEx and UPS guys will come in just to say hi (and why are they always so hot?). Neighbors you didn't know you had will knock on your door just about the time the goods are ready to come out of the oven. This is true. I swear. Don't take my word for it—open the oven door and try it for yourself.

Pumpkin Muffins

These are a favorite around these parts. We save them for the cooler seasons, but folks beg for them all year long.

Makes 12 muffins

⅓ cup non-hydrogenated vegan margarine (recommended: Earth Balance)

½ cup plus 1 ½ tablespoons (4.2 ounces) sugar

¾ cup canned pumpkin puree (not pumpkin pie mix)

½ cup soymilk

¼ cup vegetable or canola oil

2 tablespoons water

1 tablespoon molasses

1 teaspoon vanilla extract

1 cup plus 3 tablespoons (6 ounces) all-purpose flour

1 cup (5 ounces) whole wheat pastry flour

1 ½ teaspoons baking powder

½ teaspoon baking soda

1 teaspoon ground cinnamon

¼ teaspoon ground nutmeg

¼ teaspoon ground ginger

¼ teaspoon salt

¾ cup toasted pumpkin seeds, plus more for topping (optional)

Cinnamon-sugar for topping (optional)

1. Preheat the oven to 350°F.
2. Line a standard muffin tin with 12 paper liners.
3. In the bowl of a stand mixer, combine the margarine and sugar, and cream together with the paddle attachment.
4. Scrape the bottom of the bowl down and add the pumpkin puree. Mix until combined.
5. In a small bowl, whisk together the soymilk, oil, water, molasses, and vanilla. Add to the sugar mixture and mix until combined.
6. In a large bowl, combine the flours, baking powder, baking soda, cinnamon, nutmeg, ginger, and salt.

7. Add the dry ingredients to the wet ingredients until just mixed. Do not overmix the batter. Fold in the pumpkin seeds.

8. Fill the muffin cups two-thirds full. Sprinkle the top of each muffin with cinnamon-sugar and pumpkin seeds, if using.

9. Bake for 20 minutes, or until a toothpick inserted in the center of a muffin comes out clean. Leave in the pan and set it on a wire mesh rack to cool.

VARIATION: PUMPKIN LOAF

Make the batter as above. Lightly grease and flour a loaf (9 by 5-inch, or 1-pound) pan. Pour the batter in and bake for 45 minutes to 1 hour, until a toothpick inserted in the center comes out clean. If the top of your loaf starts to get too dark before the center is done, cover the pan with foil. Leave in the pan and set it on a wire mesh rack to cool.

Love Bite

Omega Fatty Acids

Omega-3s and omega-6s are essential fatty acids, the kinds you can't make on your own. You need to find sources for these luscious lubricants, and you'd better pay attention when looking for them. Most folks think simply eating fish will supply you with the amounts you need. Wrong. Farm-raised fish, the majority of what is affordable and available, is lacking in omega-3s and too high in omega-6s as a result of the diets they are fed. You desperately need both of these fatty acids, and in the appropriate amounts. Almonds, walnuts, pumpkin seeds, and flaxseeds will work to keep the omegas in balance, reduce inflammation, and help you remember where those slippery car keys are. All while you enjoy every bite.

Muffins, Breads, and Scones

Orange Cranberry Ginger Muffins

This is deliciousness in triplicate. And immensely healthy, too! The vitamin C from the crans, the hearty benefits from the ginger, and the smile they bring to your face—those benefits sure do add up!

Makes 12 muffins

2 tablespoons non-hydrogenated vegan margarine (recommended: Earth Balance)

½ cup plus 1 ½ tablespoons (4.2 ounces) sugar

2 tablespoons brown sugar

½ cup soymilk

⅓ cup vegetable or canola oil

2 tablespoons orange juice

1 teaspoon vanilla extract

1 to 2 drops orange oil, to taste

1 ½ teaspoons egg replacer (recommended: Ener-G)

¼ cup water

2 cups plus 2 tablespoons (10.6 ounces) all-purpose flour, plus more for tossing the cranberries

1 teaspoon baking powder

½ teaspoon baking soda

½ teaspoon salt

½ teaspoon ground ginger

½ cup fresh cranberries

1. Preheat the oven to 350°F.
2. Line a standard muffin tin with 12 paper liners.
3. In the bowl of a stand mixer, combine the margarine and sugars, and cream together with the paddle attachment.
4. In a small bowl, whisk together the soymilk, oil, orange juice, vanilla, and orange oil. Add to the sugar mixture and mix until combined.
5. In another small bowl, whisk together the egg replacer and water. Add to the sugar mixture and stir until combined.

6. In a large bowl, combine the 2 cups flour, baking powder, baking soda, salt, and ginger. Add to the wet ingredients until just mixed. Do not overmix the batter; the batter should be lumpy.

7. Coarsely chop the cranberries and toss them in a small amount of flour to coat. Fold in the cranberries.

8. Fill the muffin cups two-thirds full. Bake for 25 to 30 minutes, until a toothpick inserted in the center of a muffin comes out clean. Leave in the pan and set it on a wire mesh rack to cool.

VARIATION: ORANGE CRANBERRY GINGER LOAF

Make the batter as above. Lightly grease and flour a loaf (9 by 5-inch, or 1-pound) pan. Pour the batter in and bake for 45 minutes to 1 hour, until a toothpick inserted in the center comes out clean. If the top of your loaf starts to get too dark before the center is done, cover the pan with foil. Leave in the pan and set it on a wire mesh rack to cool.

Love Bite

Vitamin C

Vitamin C, or ViC, as I like to call it, is much more complex than you might realize. Most commonly known for its superb performance in fighting off what ails you, its most incredible act is the part it plays in the making of collagen, the major protein that gives structural integrity to our fibrous tissue. The basic structure of our being would be limp without ViC. Mother Nature must have known that we would be a spectacle without it and managed to sneak it into multitudes of foods. While ViC can be destroyed by cooking, not all is lost. But just to be sure we get plenty, I say encore!

Peach Almond Muffins

FYI, the recipe calls for a half cup of almonds, but if you want to add more to the top or into the batter, I won't complain, and neither will your taste buds.

Makes 12 muffins

⅓ cup plus 1 tablespoon vegetable or canola oil

⅓ cup plus 1 tablespoon soymilk

1 tablespoon silken tofu

2 tablespoons non-hydrogenated vegan cream cheese (recommended: Tofutti)

1 teaspoon almond extract

1 teaspoon vanilla extract

1 medium peach (6 ounces), pitted and chopped

⅔ cup plus 1 ½ tablespoons (4.8 ounces) sugar

2 cups (10 ounces) all-purpose flour

3 tablespoons almond flour

1 ½ teaspoons baking powder

1 ½ teaspoons baking soda

¼ teaspoon salt

½ cup sliced almonds

1. Preheat the oven to 350ºF.
2. Line a standard muffin tin with 12 paper liners.
3. In a blender, combine the oil, soymilk, tofu, cream cheese, and almond and vanilla extracts and blend until smooth.
4. In a bowl, toss the peach pieces with the sugar until they are completely coated.
5. In a large bowl, whisk together the all-purpose flour, almond flour, baking powder, baking soda, and salt. Stir in the almonds.
6. Add the soymilk mixture to the dry ingredients and stir to combine.
7. Fold in the peach mixture until everything comes together.

8. Fill the muffin cups two-thirds full. Bake for 20 minutes, or until a toothpick inserted in the center of a muffin comes out clean. Leave in pan and set on a wire mesh rack to cool.

Love Bite

Fiber

The way you process your food is a great indicator of just how healthy you are. So learning about one's constitution can really help us get down to the bottom of things. Soluble or insoluble fiber from all things vegetable is outrageously beneficial, acting like little scrub brushes in your blood and in your body. Many of the ingredients we use at Sticky Fingers have more fiber than the products you would use in traditional baking. You will be blown away by the immediate benefits, like feeling fuller faster and staying satiated longer. Every little bit counts. Getting your fiber from a variety of foods is easier on your tummy and taste buds.

Coffee Cake

This cake will turn any coffee-klatch into an outright rager. Don't be alarmed if the cops show up, 'cause this one will make your coffee cake–eating crowd make some noise!

Makes one 9-inch round cake

FOR THE TOPPING

½ cup (2.5 ounces) all-purpose flour

2 tablespoons sugar

2 tablespoons brown sugar

1 teaspoon ground cinnamon

¼ cup non-hydrogenated vegan margarine (recommended: Earth Balance)

FOR THE CAKE

1 cup soymilk

2 tablespoons lemon juice

¼ cup (1.75 ounces) sugar

¼ cup (1.75 ounces) brown sugar

1 cup plus 1 ½ tablespoons (5.5 ounces) all-purpose flour

¾ cup (3.75 ounces) whole wheat pastry flour

1 teaspoon baking powder

½ teaspoon baking soda

1 teaspoon ground cinnamon

½ teaspoon salt

⅓ cup non-hydrogenated vegan margarine (recommended: Earth Balance)

2 tablespoons vegan sour cream (recommended: Tofutti)

1 teaspoon vanilla extract

1 ½ teaspoons egg replacer (recommended: Ener-G)

¼ cup water

8 ounces fruit of choice (such as blueberries or chopped apples; optional)

1. Make the topping: In a medium bowl, combine the flour, sugars, and cinnamon.
2. Cut in the margarine and stir together with a fork until the mixture becomes crumbly. Cover and refrigerate while you mix the batter.
3. Make the cake: Preheat the oven to 350°F.
4. Grease a 9-inch round cake pan and set aside.
5. In a small bowl, combine the soymilk and lemon juice and set aside for 5 minutes to curdle.
6. In a large bowl, whisk together the sugars, flours, baking powder, baking soda, cinnamon, and salt.
7. Cut in the margarine until the mixture resembles coarse crumbs.
8. In a separate bowl, whisk together the sour cream, vanilla, egg replacer, and water until combined.
9. Add the egg replacer mixture and the curdled soymilk to the sugar mixture and stir to combine.
10. Spoon the batter into the prepared pan.
11. Top the batter with the fruit, if using. Spread the crumb topping evenly over the top. Bake for 30 minutes (50 minutes if you used the fruit), or until a toothpick inserted in the cake comes out clean.
12. Leave in pan and set on a wire mesh rack to cool.

Pecan Spice Coffee Cake

Who needs an alarm clock? You'll jump out of bed if you know this is waiting for you. And it tastes great with tea, too.

Makes one 9-inch round cake

FOR THE PECAN TOPPING

½ (2.5 ounces) cup all-purpose flour

2 tablespoons sugar

2 tablespoons brown sugar

1 teaspoon ground cinnamon

½ cup chopped pecans

¼ cup non-hydrogenated vegan margarine (recommended: Earth Balance)

FOR THE CAKE

1 cup soymilk

2 tablespoons lemon juice

¼ cup (1.75 ounces) sugar

¼ cup (1.75 ounces) brown sugar

1 cup plus 1 ½ tablespoons (5.5 ounces) all-purpose flour

¾ cup (3.75 ounces) whole wheat pastry flour

1 teaspoon baking powder

½ teaspoon baking soda

1 teaspoon ground cinnamon

½ teaspoon salt

⅓ cup non-hydrogenated vegan margarine (recommended: Earth Balance)

2 tablespoons non-hydrogenated vegan sour cream (recommended: Tofutti)

1 teaspoon vanilla extract

1 ½ teaspoons egg replacer (recommended: Ener-G)

¼ cup water

1. Make the pecan topping: In a medium bowl, combine the flour, sugars, and cinnamon. Stir in the pecans.
2. Cut in the margarine and stir together with a fork until the mixture becomes crumbly. Cover and refrigerate while you mix the batter.
3. Make the cake: Preheat the oven to 350°F.
4. Grease a 9-inch round cake pan and set aside.
5. In a small bowl, combine the soymilk and lemon juice and set aside for 5 minutes to curdle.
6. In a large bowl, whisk together the sugars, flours, baking powder, baking soda, cinnamon, and salt.
7. Cut in the margarine until the mixture resembles coarse crumbs.
8. In a separate bowl, whisk together the sour cream, vanilla, egg replacer, and water until combined.
9. Add the egg replacer mixture and the curdled soymilk to the sugar mixture and stir to combine.
10. Spoon the batter into the prepared pan.
11. Spread the crumb topping evenly over the top and bake for 30 minutes, or until a toothpick inserted in the cake comes out clean. Leave in pan and set on a wire mesh rack to cool.

Love Bite

························

You Pressed My What?

Nuts and seeds contain the healthier versions of saturated fats, the fats that are more solid at room temperature. The process in which the oils are extracted and used is called expeller-pressing or cold-pressing. They both do the same thing: They press the nuts and seeds until the oils are expelled. Cold just means the temperature is kept below 125ºF through the process so as not to disrupt the delicate chemical makeup of the raw oils. The products we use for our solid, expeller-pressed fats (Earth Balance margarine and shortening) are all-natural and non-GMO, so rest assured, you can indulge without the worry of chemicals and preservatives in your precious treats.

Orange Cranberry Scones

The more cranberries, the merrier! And orange oil and zest make for a crisp flavor. With these two you have more of a union, a marriage of sorts. This one is sure to last a lifetime in your baking rotation.

Makes 8 scones

[handwritten note: tasty! should bake longer]

½ cup non-hydrogenated vegan margarine (recommended: Earth Balance)

½ cup (3.5 ounces) sugar, plus more for sprinkling (optional)

1 teaspoon vanilla extract

⅛ teaspoon orange oil, or more to taste

2 teaspoons orange zest

⅓ cup soymilk

¾ cup plus 1 ½ tablespoons (4.2 ounces) all-purpose flour

1 ⅓ cups (6.7 ounces) whole wheat pastry flour

2 ½ teaspoons baking powder

½ teaspoon salt

¾ cup dried cranberries

1. Preheat the oven to 350°F.
2. Line a baking sheet with parchment paper.
3. In the bowl of a stand mixer, combine the margarine, ½ cup sugar, vanilla, orange oil, and orange zest and cream together with the paddle attachment until fluffy, 2 to 3 minutes.
4. With the mixer on low, slowly pour in the soymilk.
5. In a separate bowl, whisk together the flours, baking powder, and salt. Stir in the cranberries.
6. Add the dry ingredients to the wet ingredients and mix until just combined.
7. For round scones, scoop the batter onto the parchment-lined baking sheet using a 2-ounce spring-loaded ice cream scoop or a large spoon. For triangular scones, on a work surface, mold the dough into a rectangle. Cut

lengthwise and then from corner to corner, making triangles. Place the triangular pieces on the baking sheet.

8. Sprinkle the tops of the scones with granulated sugar if using, and bake for 15 minutes. The tops will look dry and the edges will be slightly brown when done. Place the baking sheet on a wire mesh rack and let cool.

Love Bite

Cranberries

We ♥ ♥ cranberries. So much so that we have cranberry goodness all year round and sneak them in everything from scones to cheesecake topping. The extra-tart flavor is a great complement to anything and everything smooth, sweet, savory, or spicy. And they might help with a few other little things like, oh, preventing cancer, slowing down the aging process, keeping bacteria from causing inflammation, and stopping dental plaque from building up. And their antioxidant qualities can help keep your heart healthy. These berries are too good to save for the holiday season— eat 'em all year long!

Chapter 7

Brownies

I love brownies: the crunchy tops, the fudgy middles, and the hidden sweet surprises, like chocolate chips and fruit. There is nothing like a great brownie. No surprise that it took years to develop and settle on a brownie everyone here at Sticky Fingers could agree upon. So after much taste-testing and batter-making, I present to you the fudgiest, most scintillating chocolaty brownies you will ever have the pleasure of eating.

Brownies

Ladies and gentlemen, please put your hands together for the boldest, brightest, and the most handsome fudgetastic brownie you will ever indulge in.

Makes 12 large or 24 small brownies

½ cup plus 2 tablespoons brewed coffee

1 tablespoon non-hydrogenated vegan margarine (recommended: Earth Balance)

3 ounces dark chocolate (58% or darker), finely chopped or pistoles

2 ¾ cups plus 1 tablespoon (1 pound, 3.6 ounces) sugar

¾ cup plus 3 tablespoons (3.75 ounces) cocoa powder

1 ½ teaspoons salt

⅔ cup vegetable or canola oil

½ cup plus 1 tablespoon water

1 tablespoon vanilla extract

2 cups plus 3 tablespoons (11 ounces) all-purpose flour

1 teaspoon baking powder

¾ cup chocolate chips

1. Preheat the oven to 350°F.
2. Grease a 9 by 13-inch baking pan.
3. Using a double boiler, heat the coffee, margarine, and dark chocolate, stirring, until the chocolate is melted and the ingredients are thoroughly combined.
4. In the bowl of a stand mixer, combine the sugar, cocoa powder, and salt and mix together with the paddle attachment.
5. Add the oil, water, and vanilla and mix to combine.
6. Add the coffee mixture and mix to combine.
7. In a separate bowl, mix together the flour and baking powder. Stir in the chocolate chips. Add the dry ingredients to the wet ingredients and mix until all the ingredients are incorporated.

8. Pour the batter into the prepared baking pan and bake for 45 to 55 minutes, until a toothpick inserted in the center comes out clean. Cool completely, then cut into squares.

S'Mores

Load 'em up! We like to pile on extra goodness, from rocky road to peanut butter pretzels. And don't forget S'Mores! You'll need a pastry torch for this.

Brownies (page 178)
1 cup chocolate chips
4 cups mini vegan marshmallows (recommended: Dandies or Sweet & Sara)
24 graham cracker squares

1. Once brownies are cooled and cut, melt ½ cup of chocolate chips in a microwave. Drizzle the melted chips over the brownies.
2. Pile the marshmallows onto the brownies, on top of the melted chips. Using a pastry torch, flame the marshmallows until you get some browning, being careful not to burn them. Sprinkle the remaining chips on top.
3. Break the graham cracker squares in half and press them into the marshmallows so that they stand upright. Or, simply crush them in a plastic bag and sprinkle them over the top.

Love Bite

Chocolate

Have you ever wondered why chocolate can pull you out of a funk? Nope, it's not the creamy texture. Not that alluring scent you can sniff out a mile away, either. It's because it contains phenylethylamine, which has a mood-elevating effect somewhat akin to amphetamine-type substances. No wonder our hearts race when we even think about the stuff. Could this be where the term "chocoholic" comes from? Good news for us vegan bakers: The milk in milk chocolate can negate some of its charming qualities, so unadulterated, dairy-free dark chocolate is your best choice.

Peppermint Brownies

I saw someone eating a brownie covered in crushed mint candy and dripping with frosting. I said to myself, "I want to eat that." And being a very convincing self, I made sure I would get what I want. For me, and for everyone to enjoy.

Makes 12 large or 24 small brownies

FOR THE BROWNIE BATTER

1/2 cup plus 2 tablespoons brewed coffee

1 tablespoon non-hydrogenated vegan margarine (recommended: Earth Balance)

3 ounces dark chocolate (58% or darker), finely chopped or pistoles

2 3/4 cups plus 1 tablespoon (1 pound, 3.6 ounces) sugar

3/4 cup plus 3 tablespoons (3.75 ounces) cocoa powder

1 1/2 teaspoons salt

2/3 cup vegetable or canola oil

2/3 cup water

1 1/2 teaspoons vanilla extract

1 1/2 teaspoons peppermint extract

2 cups plus 3 tablespoons (11 ounces) all-purpose flour

1 teaspoon baking powder

3/4 cup chocolate chips

FOR THE PEPPERMINT GLAZE

2 cups (9 ounces) powdered sugar

2 teaspoons peppermint extract

2 tablespoons water

1 cup crushed peppermint candies

1. Make the brownie batter: Preheat the oven to 350°F.
2. Grease a 9 by 13-inch baking pan.
3. Using a double boiler, heat the coffee, margarine, and dark chocolate, stirring, until the chocolate is melted and the ingredients are thoroughly combined.

4. In the bowl of a stand mixer, combine the sugar, cocoa powder, and salt and mix together with the paddle attachment.

5. Add the oil, water, and vanilla and peppermint extracts and stir to combine.

6. Add the coffee mixture and stir to combine.

7. In a separate bowl, mix together the flour and baking powder. Stir in the chocolate chips. Add the dry ingredients to the wet ingredients and mix until all the ingredients are incorporated.

8. Pour the batter into the prepared baking pan and bake for 45 to 55 minutes, until a toothpick inserted in the center comes out clean. Cool completely.

9. While the brownies are cooling, make the glaze: In a small bowl, combine the powdered sugar and peppermint extract. Slowly add the water, stirring until smooth.

10. Drizzle the brownies with the glaze and sprinkle with crushed peppermint candies.

11. Allow the glaze to set for 15 minutes before cutting into squares.

Brownies with Nuts

Don't choose one, use all of them. Combine your nuts for one serious crunch fest!

Makes 12 large or 24 small brownies

½ cup plus 2 tablespoons brewed coffee

1 tablespoon non-hydrogenated vegan margarine (recommended: Earth Balance)

3 ounces dark chocolate (58% or darker), finely chopped or pistoles

2 ¾ cups plus 1 tablespoon (1 pound, 3.6 ounces) sugar

¾ cup plus 3 tablespoons (3.75 ounces) cocoa powder

1 ½ teaspoons salt

2/3 cup vegetable or canola oil

½ cup plus 1 tablespoon water

1 tablespoon vanilla extract

2 cups plus 3 tablespoons (11 ounces) all-purpose flour

1 teaspoon baking powder

1 cup chopped nuts, such as pecans, walnuts, or almonds, plus extra for topping

1. Preheat the oven to 350°F.
2. Grease a 9 by 13-inch baking pan.
3. Using a double boiler, heat the coffee, margarine, and dark chocolate, stirring, until the chocolate is melted and the ingredients are thoroughly combined.
4. In the bowl of a stand mixer, combine the sugar, cocoa powder, and salt and cream together with the paddle attachment.
5. Add the oil, water, and vanilla and mix to combine.

6. Add the coffee mixture and mix to combine.

7. In a separate bowl, mix together the flour and baking powder. Stir in the nuts. Add the dry ingredients to the wet ingredients and mix until all the ingredients are incorporated.

8. Pour the batter into the prepared baking pan and sprinkle the top with the nuts.

9. Bake for 45 to 55 minutes, until a toothpick inserted in the center comes out clean. Cool completely before cutting into squares.

Chapter 8

Making Whoopie

Pies of whoopie will cause you to jump up and shout their name with every bite you take. These little guys have been a well-kept secret in the Northeast region. When I was a wee one, we would go to visit my cousins in New Hampshire; once my parents made the mistake of stopping into a bakery to pick up a simple little dessert for after dinner, with much emphasis on the *after*. The first thing I saw was the tray of whoopie pies. Each one looked bigger than my face (it was this big!!!). I began to salivate. My heart rate exploded as I thought, panicking, "What if they don't buy it for me? What if I never get to taste it? What if they make me leave without one?" I regained my composure as best I could, looked up at my dad with my big brown eyes, and said the very best "please, Daddy" I'd ever emitted. It was Oscar-worthy, really. In slow motion, this soft chocolaty giant filled with marshmallow crème came down to me in a halo of parchment paper, with the bakery hand of God placing it into mine. Nope, no "thank you," but rather an outright scream of exuberance. And then I proceeded to eat the whole thing before my parents could cry, "After dinner!"

Chocolate Whoopie Pies

Sumptuous simplicity at its finest.

Makes 12 large or 24 small whoopie pies

FOR THE COOKIES

1 cup soymilk

1 tablespoon vinegar (recommended: apple cider vinegar)

2 cups (10 ounces) all-purpose flour

3/4 cup (3 ounces) cocoa powder

1 teaspoon baking soda

1/2 teaspoon baking powder

1/2 teaspoon salt

1/3 cup non-hydrogenated vegan margarine (recommended: Earth Balance)

1 cup (7 ounces) sugar

1 1/2 teaspoons egg replacer (recommended: Ener-G)

2 tablespoons water

FOR THE VANILLA FILLING

1/4 cup plus 2 tablespoons non-hydrogenated vegetable shortening (recommended: Earth Balance)

2 tablespoons non-hydrogenated vegan margarine (recommended: Earth Balance)

1 1/2 cups (6.75 ounces) powdered sugar

1 teaspoon vanilla extract

1/2 to 1 tablespoon soymilk, as needed

1. Make the cookies: Preheat the oven to 350°F.
2. Line 2 baking sheets with parchment paper.
3. In a small bowl, combine the soymilk and vinegar and set aside for 5 minutes to curdle.
4. In a large bowl, whisk together the flour, cocoa powder, baking soda, baking powder, and salt and set aside.

5. In the bowl of a stand mixer, combine the margarine and sugar, and cream together with the paddle attachment until light and fluffy, 2 to 3 minutes. Scrape the sides and bottom of the bowl and mix on high speed to ensure that all the ingredients are incorporated, about 1 minute more.

6. In a small bowl, whisk together the egg replacer and water. Add to the sugar mixture and mix until thoroughly combined.

7. Add half of the dry ingredients, then all of the curdled soymilk. Add the remaining dry ingredients and mix to combine. Do not overmix.

8. Using a spring-loaded ice cream scoop, scoop mounds of dough (24 for large or 48 for small pies) about 1 inch apart on the prepared baking sheets. Use a 1-ounce scoop for small pies or a 2-ounce scoop for large.

9. Bake until the cookies spring back to the touch or a toothpick inserted into the center of a cookie comes out clean, 8 to 10 minutes, rotating the pans halfway through baking. Let cool completely on the pans.

10. Make the vanilla filling: In the bowl of a stand mixer, combine the shortening and margarine and whip with the paddle attachment until completely combined. Scrape the bottom of the bowl to ensure that the ingredients are mixed thoroughly.

11. On low speed, slowly add the powdered sugar a little at a time.

12. Add the vanilla, then add the soymilk, and mix on low until the liquids are incorporated and the desired consistency is reached. Scrape the bottom of the bowl and mix on medium-high speed until all the ingredients are combined and the filling is fluffy, about 2 minutes.

13. To assemble: Fill a pastry bag with the filling. Pipe a dollop of filling on the flat (bottom) side of half of the cooled cookies. Top with the remaining cookies, flat side down, pressing down slightly so the filling spreads to the edges of the cookies.

Vanilla Whoopie Pies

Sometimes you have to make a scene to prove your point. The vanilla whoopie does that. Seemingly reserved and a bit of a wallflower, vanilla doesn't appear as daring as all those bold flavors. Look out! Vanilla has something to prove, and she's about to win you over.

Makes 10 large or 20 small whoopie pies

2 ¼ cups (11.2 ounces) all-purpose flour

¾ teaspoon baking powder

¼ teaspoon baking soda

½ teaspoon salt

½ cup non-hydrogenated vegan margarine (recommended: Earth Balance)

1 cup (7 ounces) brown sugar

1 ½ teaspoons egg replacer (recommended: Ener-G)

2 tablespoons water

1 teaspoon vanilla extract

1 cup soymilk

Vanilla Filling (page 186)

1. Preheat the oven to 350°F.
2. Line 2 baking sheets with parchment paper.
3. In a large bowl, whisk together the flour, baking powder, baking soda, and salt.
4. In the bowl of a stand mixer, combine the margarine and brown sugar, and cream together with the whisk attachment until light and fluffy, 2 to 3 minutes. Scrape the bottom of the bowl to ensure that the ingredients are incorporated.
5. In a small bowl, whisk together the egg replacer and water.
6. Add the egg replacer mixture and vanilla to the sugar mixture and mix until well combined.
7. With the mixer on low, beat in the flour mixture in three additions, alternating with the soymilk and ending with the flour mixture and scraping the bowl as needed. Beat until combined; do not overmix.

8. Using a spring-loaded ice cream scoop, scoop mounds of dough (20 for large or 40 for small pies) about 1 inch apart on the prepared baking sheets. Use a 1-ounce scoop for small pies or a 2-ounce scoop for large.

9. Bake until the cookies puff up and the edges are golden or a toothpick inserted into the center of a cookie comes out clean, 17 to 19 minutes, rotating the trays halfway through baking. Let cool completely on the pans while you make the filling.

10. To assemble: Fill a pastry bag with the filling. Pipe a large dollop of filling on the flat (bottom) side of half of the cooled cookies. Top with the remaining cookies, pressing down slightly so that the filling spreads to the edges of the cookies.

Love Bite

Cravings

Why do we crave that special something even if we aren't hungry? Is there some sixth sense scientists haven't discovered, one that forces us to long for the magic ingredient in cupcakes, chips, or pasta that will cure what ails us? Or is it that we desire our favorite foods, the ones we rarely eat and that usually have the most calories? Scientists may never know, because delving into the depths of cravings means studying humans as subjects, a difficult group to control. Forcing folks to go without and fight the urge will never be a popular research study or one with many willing subjects. It's not even very feasible as long-term research, as everyone would quit after the first day (I know I would). One thing we do know here at Sticky Fingers is that giving in to those cravings (in moderation) will make you happier and much nicer to be around.

Peanut Butter Banana Whoopie Pies

You know you want to. Come on, with me, as loud as you can: "Whoopie!!"

Makes 12 large or 24 small whoopie pies

FOR THE COOKIES

2 cups (10 ounces) all-purpose flour

½ teaspoon baking powder

½ teaspoon baking soda

½ teaspoon salt

½ cup mashed banana (from 1 large ripe banana)

½ cup vegan sour cream (recommended: Tofutti)

½ cup non-hydrogenated vegan margarine (recommended: Earth Balance)

½ cup (3.5 ounces) sugar

½ cup (3.5 ounces) packed light brown sugar

1 teaspoon vanilla extract

1 ½ teaspoons egg replacer (recommended: Ener-G)

2 tablespoons water

FOR THE PEANUT BUTTER FILLING

1 ¾ cups smooth peanut butter (recommended: Skippy Natural)

⅔ cup non-hydrogenated vegetable shortening (recommended: Earth Balance)

⅔ cup non-hydrogenated vegan margarine (recommended: Earth Balance)

4 cups (1 pound, 2 ounces) powdered sugar

½ cup soymilk

1. Preheat the oven to 350°F.

2. Line 2 baking sheets with parchment paper.

3. In a large bowl, whisk together the flour, baking powder, baking soda, and salt.

4. In another bowl, mix together the banana and sour cream.

5. In the bowl of a stand mixer, combine the margarine, sugars, and vanilla and cream with the paddle attachment until light and fluffy, 2 to 3 minutes.

6. In a small bowl, whisk together the egg replacer and water. Add to the sugar mixture and mix until well combined.

7. Add the banana mixture in two additions, alternating with the dry ingredients, and mix to combine. Do not overmix.

8. Using a spring-loaded ice cream scoop, scoop mounds of batter (24 for large or 48 for small pies) about 1 inch apart on the prepared baking sheets. Use a 1-ounce scoop for small pies or a 2-ounce scoop for large.

9. Bake until the cookies puff up and the edges of the cookies are golden or a toothpick inserted into the center of a cookie comes out clean, 12 to 14 minutes, rotating the pans halfway through baking. Let cool completely on the pans.

10. Make the filling: In the bowl of a stand mixer, combine the peanut butter, shortening, and margarine and whip until light and fluffy, 5 to 7 minutes.

11. Scrape the bottom of the bowl to ensure that all the ingredients are mixed thoroughly.

12. On low speed, slowly add the powdered sugar a little at a time.

13. Add the soymilk and mix on low speed until the liquid is incorporated.

14. Scrape the bottom of the bowl and mix on medium-high speed until all the ingredients are combined and the filling is fluffy, about 2 minutes.

15. To assemble: Fill a pastry bag with the filling. Pipe a dollop of filling on the flat (bottom) side of half of the cooled cookies.

16. Top with the remaining cookies, pressing down slightly so the filling spreads to the edges of the cookies.

Love Bite

....

Mixing Burns Calories

Unless you pick up a 1940s guide to homemaking, you probably won't see a source for the number of calories burned during ironing, baking, or martini-making. But rest assured, your mixing is a calorie absolver, which will redeem itself during the last steps in recipe-making: indulging.

Strawberry Lemonade Whoopie Pies

Y ou will be delightfully confused when you taste these whoopie pies. Your mouth will say "juicy," but your eyes will say "whoopie pie."

Makes 18 large or 36 small whoopie pies

FOR THE COOKIES

3 ¼ cups plus 2 ½ tablespoons (1 pound, 1 ounce) all-purpose flour

1 teaspoon baking powder

½ teaspoon baking soda

1 cup non-hydrogenated vegan margarine (recommended: Earth Balance)

2 cups (14 ounces) sugar

1 tablespoon egg replacer (recommended: Ener-G)

¼ cup water

Zest of 1 lemon

⅔ cup lemon juice

1 teaspoon vinegar (recommended: apple cider)

FOR THE STRAWBERRY FILLING

¼ cup plus 2 tablespoons non-hydrogenated vegetable shortening (recommended: Earth Balance)

2 tablespoons non-hydrogenated vegan margarine (recommended: Earth Balance)

½ cup strawberry puree (store-bought or homemade; see Note, page 40)

1 ½ cups (6.75 ounces) powdered sugar

1 ½ teaspoons lemon juice

1. Make the cookies: Preheat the oven to 350°F.
2. Line 2 baking sheets with parchment paper.
3. In a large bowl, whisk together the flour, baking powder, and baking soda.

4. In the bowl of a stand mixer, combine the margarine and sugar, and cream with the paddle attachment until light and fluffy, about 2 minutes. Scrape the sides and bottom of the bowl.

5. In a small bowl, whisk together the egg replacer and water.

6. Add the egg replacer mixture and lemon zest to the sugar mixture and mix until well combined.

7. Combine the lemon juice and vinegar and add to the sugar mixture, alternating with the dry ingredients until all is added. Mix until incorporated. Do not overmix.

8. Using a spring-loaded ice cream scoop, scoop mounds of dough (36 for large or 72 for small pies) about 1 inch apart on the prepared baking sheets. Use a 1-ounce scoop for small pies or a 2-ounce scoop for large.

9. Bake until the cookies are just starting to crack on top and a toothpick inserted into the center of a cookie comes out clean, about 15 minutes. Let cool completely on the pans.

10. Make the filling: In the bowl of a stand mixer, combine the shortening and margarine and whip until completely combined. Scrape the bottom of the bowl to ensure that the ingredients are mixed thoroughly.

11. Add the strawberry puree and mix until incorporated. Scrape the bottom of the bowl.

12. On low speed, slowly add the powdered sugar a little at a time.

13. Add the lemon juice and mix to combine. Scrape the bottom of the bowl and mix on medium-high speed until all the ingredients are combined and the filling is fluffy, about 2 minutes.

14. To assemble, fill a pastry bag with the filling. Pipe a dollop of filling on the flat (bottom) side of half of the cooled cookies. Top with the remaining cookies, pressing down slightly so the filling spreads to the edges of the cookies.

Pumpkin Whoopie Pies

One year around October, as we were gearing up for the fall season, I suddenly decided we needed more options for the holidays. Something fun and new, something no one would expect. We all got to work contemplating what would be our next creation, and Ramon, baker extraordinaire, with a bit of help from Kamber, the fancy pants specialty cake decorator, came up with what has become our most sought-after holiday item.

Makes 24 large or 48 small whoopie pies

FOR THE COOKIES

3 cups (15 ounces) all-purpose flour

1 teaspoon salt

1 teaspoon baking powder

1 teaspoon baking soda

1 tablespoon ground cinnamon

2 teaspoons ground ginger

1 teaspoon ground cloves

½ teaspoon ground nutmeg

½ teaspoon ground allspice

2 cups (14 ounces) packed brown sugar

1 cup vegetable or canola oil

3 cups canned pumpkin puree (not pumpkin pie filling)

1 tablespoon egg replacer (recommended: Ener-G)

¼ cup water

1 teaspoon vanilla extract

FOR THE CREAM CHEESE FILLING

⅓ cup non-hydrogenated vegetable shortening (recommended: Earth Balance)

4 ounces non-hydrogenated vegan cream cheese (recommended: Tofutti), softened

1 ½ cups (6.75 ounces) powdered sugar

1 teaspoon vanilla extract

½ teaspoon lemon juice

1 to 2 drops lemon oil, to taste

1. Preheat the oven to 350°F.

2. Line 2 baking sheets with parchment paper.

3. In a large bowl, whisk together the flour, salt, baking powder, baking soda, cinnamon, ginger, cloves, nutmeg, and allspice.

4. In the bowl of a stand mixer, combine the brown sugar and oil and mix with the paddle attachment until well combined.

5. Add the pumpkin puree and mix until combined.

6. In a small bowl, whisk together the egg replacer and water.

7. Add the egg replacer mixture and vanilla to the pumpkin mixture and mix until well combined.

8. Add the flour mixture to the pumpkin mixture, about 1 cup at a time, and mix until fully incorporated.

9. Using a spring-loaded ice cream scoop, scoop mounds of dough (48 for large or 96 for small pies) about 1 inch apart on the prepared baking sheets. Use a 1-ounce scoop for small pies or a 2-ounce scoop for large.

10. Transfer to the oven and bake until the cookies are just starting to crack on top and a toothpick inserted into the center of each cookie comes out clean, about 15 minutes. Let cool completely on the pans.

11. Make the filling: In the bowl of a stand mixer fitted with the paddle attachment, beat the shortening until smooth.

12. Add the cream cheese and beat until well combined.

13. Add the sugar, vanilla, lemon juice, and lemon oil and beat just until smooth. (The filling can be made in advance. Cover and refrigerate; let stand at room temperature to soften before using.)

14. To assemble: Fill a pastry bag with the filling. Pipe a dollop of filling on the flat (bottom) side of half of the cooled cookies. Top with the remaining cookies, pressing down slightly so the filling spreads to the edges of the cookies.

Love Bite

Cinnamon

Spice it up to cure your wandering ways! It's believed that seductive cinnamon can improve focus and concentration, helping you to stay engaged and on top of the task at hand. Long-term relationships are most rewarding, and being able to commit to this recipe surely will bring happiness and content. I recommend a dose of cinnamon before you begin every recipe to stay focused and to keep your eye on the prize.

Chapter 9

Fab and Fruity Pies and Cheesecakes

Pie. The very word conjures thoughts of sweet simplicity. Colorful scenes of fruit-filled crusts and crème-covered pie shells dance in your mind. The thought provokes flavor memories, and you can't hold back the crave train. You can taste their loveliness, imagine the aroma, and feel the nostalgia on your tongue. Thinking about pies is almost like indulging in pure food porn, nearly inappropriate for family-friendly cookbooks. Nearly, I said.

Fruit Pies

Fact: Pies are harder to make than you might think. Simple ingredients, check. Seemingly simple directions, check. Achievable accuracy, check. Wait a minute . . . think about it: perfectly flaky crust? Tart with just the right amount of sweet? It's hard work making perfect pie! For me, these are the most difficult recipes to execute simply because of the crust.

A perfect crumb for a crust is a delicate balance. The crumbs are bigger than you may realize and will make you nervous. Rarely do we allow for chunks of margarine and quarter-size balls of dough! But when making a flaky pie crust, those big chunks of margarine are exactly what we need, which is super-hard for all of us who love to mix and mix our batter.

And the fruit, oh the fruit! How can we be sure our baking times will preserve their tenderness without being squishy but also ensuring we won't have unchewable fruity bits? Thinking about pies gives me anxiety. The only thing that centers me and keeps me going is remembering how much I love to eat them.

Simple as Pie Crust

The easiest pie crust there is. Foolproof, as long as you don't burn it. Carry on.

Makes one 9-inch pie shell

6 tablespoons non-hydrogenated vegan margarine (recommended:
   Earth Balance)
1 ½ cups finely ground graham cracker crumbs
¼ cup (1.75 ounces) sugar

1. Preheat the oven to 350°F.
2. In a small, heavy-bottomed saucepan, melt the margarine.
3. In a large bowl, combine the graham cracker crumbs and sugar.
4. Add the melted margarine and stir to combine.
5. Press the crust mixture into a 9-inch springform pan or glass pie dish, making sure the mixture is pressed evenly across the bottom of the pan or dish. Do not push the crust up the sides of the springform.
6. Bake for 8 to 10 minutes. Cool completely before using.

Love Bite

....

Saturated Fat

While trolling around nutrition and fitness websites, I came upon the following excerpt from a book by doctors Mary Dan Eades and Michael R. Eades called *The Six-Week Cure for the Middle-Aged Middle*. Check out the two plant-source-based suggestions: "Responsible for proper nerve signaling, certain saturated fats, particularly those found in butter, lard, coconut oil, and palm oil, function directly as signaling messengers that influence metabolism, including such critical jobs such as the appropriate release of insulin."

Say what? Yep, it's true, saturated fat is actually necessary. I was excited to find out that there is yet another reason to enjoy what you eat without hesitation. No, I don't love the part about lard and butter (there is a scientifically proven truth to the term "lard ass"). I use these lifestyle books as I do the Bible; I take what I can use, apply it to my life, and enjoy the rest as a good story.

Double Sweet as Pie Crust

Use this double crust for pies with plain or lattice tops. Polite reminder: Please don't overmix your crust, as it will result in a crispy cracker rather than a flaky crust. We suggest a food processer to control the exact amount of times this mixture goes for a whirl.

Makes one 9-inch double-crust pie shell or two 9-inch single-crust shells

2 cups (10 ounces) all-purpose flour

¼ cup plus 1 tablespoon (2.25 ounces) sugar

½ teaspoon salt

2/3 cup non-hydrogenated vegan margarine (recommended: Earth Balance), chilled and cut into ¼-inch pieces

3 tablespoons cold water

1. In a food processor fitted with the metal blade, pulse together the flour, sugar, and salt until combined.
2. Add the margarine pieces and pulse 5 to 7 times, until the mixture is crumbly.
3. Add the cold water and pulse 5 to 7 more times, until the mixture just comes together.
4. Turn the dough out onto a clean work surface. Briefly knead the dough until all the dry ingredients are incorporated, about 30 seconds. Do not overmix or overknead the dough; the pie crust will be tough if you work it too long.
5. If you do not have a food processor, work the margarine into the flour mixture with a dough cutter or 2 forks. Sprinkle 1 tablespoon of the water over one-third of the mixture and gently toss with a fork. Push that moistened section of dough to the side of the bowl so you don't mix it again. Repeat this process twice more, adding 1 tablespoon of water at a time until all the dough is moist and you can form it into a ball. Do not knead it.
6. Wrap the dough tightly in plastic wrap and refrigerate until ready to use.

Single Sweet as Pie Crust

U se this crust for simple pies that top themselves.

Makes one 9-inch pie shell

1 cup (5 ounces) all-purpose flour

2 1/2 tablespoons sugar

1/4 teaspoon salt

1/3 cup non-hydrogenated vegan margarine (recommended: Earth Balance), chilled and cut into 1/4-inch pieces

1 1/2 tablespoons cold water

1. In a food processor fitted with the metal blade, pulse together the flour, sugar, and salt until combined.

2. Add the margarine pieces and pulse 5 to 7 times, until the mixture is crumbly.

3. Add the cold water and pulse 5 to 7 more times, until the mixture just comes together.

4. Turn the dough out onto a clean work surface. Briefly knead the dough until all the dry ingredients are incorporated, about 30 seconds. Do not overmix or overknead the dough; the pie crust will be tough if you work it too long.

5. If you do not have a food processor, work the margarine into the flour mixture with a dough cutter or 2 forks. Sprinkle the water over the mixture and gently toss with a fork, until all the dough is moist and you can form it into a ball. Be careful not to overmix it, and do not knead it.

6. Wrap the dough tightly in plastic wrap and refrigerate until ready to use.

Apple Pie

Nothing says "I love you" like a homemade apple pie. Or "I like you a lot." Or "I love pie and I want you to take some so I don't eat it all in one sitting." Don't underestimate the power of pie.

Makes one 9-inch pie

1 recipe Double Sweet as Pie Crust
   (page 203)
1 cup (7 ounces) sugar
¼ cup (1.25 ounces) all-purpose
   flour
1 ½ teaspoons ground cinnamon
1 teaspoon ground nutmeg

⅛ teaspoon salt
8 apples (about 3 pounds), peeled,
   cored, and chopped
2 tablespoons non-hydrogenated
   vegan margarine (recommended:
   Earth Balance), chilled and cut
   into ¼-inch pieces

1. Preheat the oven to 425°F.
2. Lightly grease a 9-inch pie pan that's at least 1 ½ inches deep.
3. Roll half of the pie dough out to a 13-inch circle and fit it into the pan. Press the dough evenly into the pan. Cut the excess crust at the rim. Refrigerate the crust and the remaining half of the dough.
4. In a large bowl, combine the sugar, flour, cinnamon, nutmeg, and salt. Add the apples and toss to completely coat.
5. Place the prepared pie pan on a baking sheet lined with parchment paper. Pour the apple filling into the unbaked pie shell, making a mound in the center. Pour over any liquid that remains in the bowl. Dot the filling with the margarine pieces.
6. Roll out the other half of the pie dough to a 13-inch circle. Place the circle over the top of the pie, cut off excess, and decoratively crimp the edges to seal the pie.

7. Cut four 1-inch slits into the top of the crust to allow steam to escape during baking.

8. Cover the edge of the crust with foil and bake for 30 minutes.

9. Remove the foil and bake for 20 minutes more, or until the edges begin to brown. Remove the pie from the oven and cool on a cooling rack for at least 4 hours before serving.

Blueberry Pie

You are about to enjoy a sweet piece of not so humble pie.

Makes one 9-inch pie

1 recipe Double Sweet as Pie Crust (page 203)

1 pint fresh blueberries

¼ cup plus 3 tablespoons sugar

2 tablespoons all-purpose flour

1 tablespoon lemon juice

1 teaspoon lemon zest

½ teaspoon vanilla extract

1 teaspoon ground cinnamon

1. Lightly grease a 9-inch pie pan that's at least 1 ½ inches deep.
2. Roll half of the pie dough out to a 13-inch circle and fit it into the pan.
3. Press the dough evenly into the pan and crimp the edges above the rim. Refrigerate the crust and the remaining half of the dough while you preheat the oven to 400°F.
4. In a large bowl, stir together the blueberries, sugar, 6 tablespoons of the flour, lemon juice, lemon zest, and vanilla. Let rest for 15 minutes to allow the blueberries to release their juices, then stir again to combine the ingredients.
5. Place the prepared pie pan on a baking sheet lined with parchment paper. Pour the blueberry filling into the unbaked pie shell.
6. Create a lattice on top of the pie with the strips and crimp the edges to seal the pie (see next step). Or simply roll out the rest of the pie crust, place on top of filled pie, crimp edges and slice a cut in the center for steam to come out. Cover the edges of the crust with foil and bake for 20 to 25 minutes.
7. To create the lattice top, roll out the other half of the pie dough to a 13-inch circle and cut it into ½-inch strips.
8. Moisten the edge of the pie, after dipping your fingers in a little bit of water. Lay the two longest strips in an X in the center of the pie. Alternate

horizontal and vertical strips, weaving them in an over-under pattern. Use the short strips for the edges. Press the ends of the strips to the edge of the pie and cut with kitchen shears or a knife. Now crimp the edges to make them look pretty. Dust the top with 1 teaspoon of cinnamon and 1 tablespoon of sugar for extra bling.

9. Cover the edges of the crust with foil and bake for 20 minutes.

10. Remove the foil and bake for 5 minutes more, or until the edges begin to brown.

11. Take the pie out of the oven and cool on a cooling rack for a minimum of 4 hours before serving.

Strawberry Rhubarb Pie with Crumb Topping

There is this awesome pie shop outside of Albany, New York (of all places), that can truly make an awesome pie. They made strawberry rhubarb especially for me, and all vegan. I swore to unlock the secrets to this masterpiece. Turns out, this is an easy one! The only thing different from your old-fashioned strawberry rhubarb pie is one simple, small ingredient we swapped out for a kinder alternative. But trust me; you won't even know it's gone. See if you can figure it out.

Makes one 9-inch pie

1 recipe Single Sweet as Pie Crust (page 204)

FOR THE FILLING
1 ¼ cups (8.75 ounces) sugar
¼ cup tapioca starch
3 ½ cups hulled and halved strawberries
3 ½ cups 1-inch rhubarb slices
Juice of ½ lime

FOR THE PISTACHIO CRUMB TOPPING
½ cup (3.5 ounces) brown sugar
½ cup (2.5 ounces) all-purpose flour, plus more if necessary
½ cup finely chopped pistachios
½ cup non-hydrogenated vegan margarine (recommended: Earth Balance), chilled and cut into ¼-inch pieces

1. Lightly grease a 9-inch pie pan that's at least 1 ½ inches deep.
2. Roll the pie dough out to a 13-inch circle and fit it into the pie pan. Press the

dough evenly into the bottom and along the sides of the pan and crimp the edges above the rim.

3. Refrigerate the crust while you preheat the oven to 450°F. Place a baking sheet in the oven to preheat.

4. Make the filling: In a large bowl, combine the sugar and tapioca starch.

5. Add the strawberries and rhubarb and toss to coat.

6. Add the lime juice and stir to combine. Set aside while you prepare the crumb topping.

7. Make the topping: In a medium bowl, mix together the brown sugar, flour, and pistachios.

8. Cut the cold margarine into the mixture until large crumbs form.

9. Pour the filling into the unbaked pie shell and sprinkle the crumb topping evenly over the fruit.

10. Place the pie on the preheated baking sheet and bake for 10 minutes.

11. Reduce the oven temperature to 350°F and bake for an additional hour, or until the crust and crumb topping are nicely browned and thick bubbles form around the fruit. If the edges of the crust begin to brown too quickly, cover the edges with aluminum foil or a pie crust shield.

12. Allow the pie to cool on a cooling rack for a minimum of 4 hours before serving.

Sweet-n-Salty Cookies, page 135

Orange Cranberry Scones, page 175

S'Mores brownie, page 179

Strawberry Lemonade Whoopie Pie, page 193

Blueberry Pie, page 207

Apple Ravioli, page 212

Banana Nut Cheesecake, page 221

Key Lime Pie, page 244

Love Bite

Rhubarb

Once upon a time rhubarb sold for over twice the price of opium. Okay, so it's been downgraded a bit since 1657 and has become much more affordable for pie making. And it contains calcium, vitamin C, and fiber, which makes it nearly priceless. Some studies show it may be healing to the lungs, may aid in avoiding allergies, and help fight cancer. Health food or just health helper, no one is sure. But it is pretty tasty paired with strawberries in this pie. Be sure to cut off all the leaves from the rhubarb stalks, as they are extremely poisonous. Keep them away from pets, kids, and anyone you would like to have around for a while. They are that poisonous, which is why they are usually sold without the leaves (phew!).

Apple Ravioli

Pockets of apple pie that fit perfectly in any size hand. Breakfast or snack, any handy handheld pie is always a crowd pleaser.

Makes 12 ravioli

FOR THE CINNAMON SUGAR

1 ½ teaspoons sugar

1 ½ teaspoons ground cinnamon

FOR THE RAVIOLI FILLING

2 teaspoons evaporated cane sugar

1 teaspoon brown sugar

2 teaspoons all-purpose flour

½ teaspoon ground cinnamon

½ teaspoon ground allspice

½ teaspoon grated nutmeg

½ teaspoon ground ginger

¼ teaspoon salt

1 tablespoon non-hydrogenated vegan margarine (recommended: Earth Balance)

2 to 3 small apples, peeled, cored, and finely chopped

2 teaspoons lemon juice

¼ teaspoon vanilla extract

2 recipes Double Sweet as Pie Crust (page 203)

1. Preheat the oven to 350ºF.
2. Make the cinnamon sugar: In a small bowl, stir together the sugar and cinnamon. Set aside.
3. Make the filling: In a large bowl, combine the sugars, flour, cinnamon, allspice, nutmeg, ginger, and salt.
4. Cut in the margarine until the mixture is crumbly.
5. Add the apples, lemon juice, and vanilla and stir until all of the apples are coated.

6. Place half (about 1 pound) of the pie crust between 2 sheets of parchment paper and roll out to a 12 by 12-inch square. Set aside.

7. Repeat with the remaining half of the pie dough.

8. Scoop 1 tablespoon of the apple mixture in rows on 1 sheet of the dough, leaving 1 inch of space between each scoop. You should have 3 rows of 4 scoops when you are finished.

9. Place the second sheet of dough on top and press the dough down between each scoop of apples to seal the crust around the mounds. Do the same along the edges of the dough.

10. Cut the sheets into 3 by 4-inch squares so that you have 12 ravioli that are the same size. Make sure each ravioli square is sealed on all sides. You can crimp the edges together with the tines of a fork to make them look pretty and to ensure a good seal.

11. Place the ravioli squares on a baking sheet lined with parchment paper and bake for 18 to 25 minutes, until the ravioli begins to brown.

12. Remove from the oven and immediately sprinkle the tops of the ravioli with cinnamon sugar. Let cool slightly before serving. This ravioli goes great with ice cream!

Bourbon Pecan Pie

An alcoholic twist on a Southern tradition. Rather than matching the dessert to the libations, I efficiently and surreptitiously work the two of them together. Sure to be the belle of any ball.

Makes one 9-inch pie

1 recipe Single Sweet as Pie
Crust (page 204)
¼ cup non-hydrogenated vegan
margarine (recommended:
Earth Balance)
⅓ cup (1.9 ounces) all-purpose
flour
½ cup bourbon

⅔ cup water
1 cup plus 1 tablespoon maple
syrup
½ cup (3.5 ounces) lightly packed
brown sugar
½ teaspoon salt
1 tablespoon vanilla extract
2 ¼ cups pecan halves

1. Lightly grease a 9-inch pie pan that's at least 1 ½ inches deep.
2. Roll the pie dough out to a 13-inch circle and fit it into the pan. Press the dough evenly into the bottom and sides of the pie dish. Crimp the edges above the rim; this will give you a little extra headroom to hold the filling when it expands in the oven.
3. Refrigerate the crust while you preheat the oven to 350°F.
4. In a medium, heavy-bottomed saucepan, melt the margarine over medium heat.
5. Add the flour and whisk until the flour is light to golden brown in color, about 5 minutes.
6. Add the bourbon and cook for 3 more minutes, stirring occasionally.
7. Stir in the water and cook for 10 minutes, stirring occasionally.

8. Stir in the maple syrup, brown sugar, and salt and continue to cook for 15 minutes, or until the mixture begins to thicken.

9. Remove from the heat and add the vanilla and pecans; stir to combine.

10. Place the prepared pie pan on a baking sheet lined with parchment paper. Pour the filling into the unbaked pie shell.

11. Bake for 15 to 20 minutes, or until crust begins to brown. Cool completely on a cooling rack.

Cheesecakes

Cheesecake is no joke. Especially when you are an Italian Jew from New York. It's at every holiday table, birthday, wedding—it's seriously everywhere! And you can't get away with a frozen grocery store-bought cake, even if you're in a major pinch. No, you have to make it yourself or go to one of the actual dealers, and there are few legit sources to speak of. So cheesecake is important, and I have high standards. As do my friends and family. They warned me not to dare try.

Which is why I was so grateful when someone else did the work for us at Sticky Fingers! I know, scandalous. But when you find a good thing, you should honor it and eat it often. So we did. And unlike so many others, we're honest about it.

We played with numerous recipes over the years. And one day, I stumbled upon some recipes from a vegan cheesecake maker hailing from Nebraska. Gasp! "How could they know a good cheesecake?" I thought. "Do they have anything other than Velveeta in the vast Midwest?" I pondered, and then decided to be the judge. I placed an order online right then and there.

After tasting these delicious creamy creations born from the land of corn, I became a believer: Even someone from outside the Big Apple can know what cheesecake is supposed to be. This vegan cheesecake goddess was a well-kept secret, but, sadly, she has since closed up shop. So I bought up the recipes and dared to try my own hand at making these midwestern marvels. A few tweaks were made here and minor little adjustments made there, and those recipes became the ones we use at Sticky Fingers. Sefika Sayood, the mastermind who imagined Delicious Choices way back when, we salute you. A big giant thank-you for paving the way and letting others build off of your genius.

Note to cheesecake makers: All recipes ask you to use a springform pan and a water bath. You may also opt for a 9- or 10-inch glass pie dish. You do not need a water bath for the pie dish if you go that route, FYI, though baking in a springform pan using the water bath method makes for a more evenly baked confection—no dry spots or runny middles. We highly recommend this method. Save the pie dishes for the pies!

Basic Cheesecake

Learn this recipe and you will want for nothing. "Deprivation" is a dirty word as far as we are concerned, especially when it comes to cheesecake.

Makes one 9-inch cheesecake

1 recipe Simple as Pie Crust (page 201), prebaked

2 cups non-hydrogenated vegan cream cheese (recommended: Tofutti), softened

2 cups vegan sour cream (recommended: Tofutti)

1 cup (7 ounces) sugar

1 ½ tablespoons egg replacer (recommended: Ener-G)

½ cup water

1 ½ teaspoons vanilla extract

½ teaspoon orange zest

½ teaspoon lemon zest

½ cup all-purpose (2.5 ounces) flour

1. Preheat the oven to 350ºF.
2. Line the sides of the prepared springform pan with a 2-inch strip of parchment paper.
3. In the bowl of a stand mixer, mix the cream cheese with the paddle attachment until soft and smooth, about 3 minutes.
4. Add the sour cream and mix to combine.
5. Add the sugar and beat until fluffy, 3 more minutes.
6. In a small bowl, whisk together the egg replacer and water.
7. Add the egg replacer mixture, vanilla, orange zest, and lemon zest to the cream cheese mixture and mix until thoroughly combined.
8. Add the flour and mix until smooth.
9. Wrap the bottom of the springform pan with aluminum foil to prevent leaks.
10. Pour the filling into the prepared pie crust.
11. Place the pan inside a deep baking dish that is a few inches larger than the springform pan.

12. Fill the baking dish with enough hot water to reach halfway up the springform pan.

13. Carefully place the pan in the oven and bake for 1 to 1 ½ hours, until the cake rises slightly and begins pulling away from the sides of the pan. The middle will be shiny and not set but will firm up as it cools.

14. Carefully remove the pan from the water bath and cool completely on a cooling rack.

15. Cover with plastic and refrigerate the cheesecake until completely chilled, at least 8 hours or overnight, then open the springform and remove the strip of parchment before serving.

Love Bite

Fat

Hey, all you fat-phobes, nutty naysayers, and oil-haters, get over here! I have GREAT news for you! Remember the "fat makes you fat" campaign of the nineties, the one that left us feeling extremely misinformed, with one huge case of post-traumatic stress disorder, and dry hair and skin to boot (among other things)? Get this, those folks were wrong! I know, I can't stop crying tears of joy, either. And the fats found in vegetables, grains, nuts, and seeds? They are the "good" fats, the ones that help lower cholesterol and keep you healthy, the fats that are liquid at room temperature (oils), or awfully close (such as coconut and palm fruit oil). Thank goodness they taste so good, or we'd be calling them health foods—gasp!

New York Cheesecake Cupcakes

After a few months of eating vegan, I suddenly felt like something was missing, but I couldn't exactly put my finger on it. And then the crave hit me like a subway train—I missed cheesecake. And not any old cheesecake, New York City cheesecake. Eating cheesecake was like a birthright. How could it suddenly be gone? Turns out it was always right under my nose. Rest assured this will calm any New York–size cheesecake cravings.

Makes 12 cupcakes

FOR THE CRUST

1 ½ cups (6 ounces) almond flour

¾ cup (5.25 ounces) sugar

½ teaspoon almond extract

2 tablespoons non-hydrogenated vegan margarine (recommended: Earth Balance)

FOR THE FILLING

2 cups non-hydrogenated vegan cream cheese (recommended: Tofutti), softened

2 cups vegan sour cream (recommended: Tofutti)

½ cup (3.5 ounces) sugar

2 teaspoons egg replacer (recommended: Ener-G)

¼ cup water

1 teaspoon vanilla extract

¼ teaspoon lemon zest

¼ teaspoon orange zest

¼ cup (1.25 ounces) all-purpose flour

1. Preheat the oven to 350°F.
2. Line one 12-cup cupcake tin with liners.

3. Make the crust: In a medium bowl, mix together the almond flour, the sugar, and the almond extract.

4. In a small, heavy-bottomed saucepan, melt the margarine. Add the melted margarine to the sugar mixture and stir to combine.

5. Fill the cupcake cups with 2 tablespoons of the crust mixture each and press the mixture into the bottom of the cupcake cups. Set aside while you make the filling.

6. Make the filling: In the bowl of a stand mixer, whip the cream cheese with a paddle attachment until soft, 1 to 2 minutes.

7. Scrape down the sides and bottom of the bowl and add the sour cream and sugar.

8. Cream together the ingredients until fluffy, 3 to 5 minutes.

9. In a small bowl, whisk together the egg replacer and water to dissolve the egg replacer. Add the egg replacer mixture to the sugar mixture and mix until incorporated.

10. Add the vanilla, lemon zest, and orange zest and mix until incorporated. Scrape down the sides and bottom of the bowl to ensure that all the ingredients are mixed together.

11. Add the flour and mix.

12. Fill the prepared almond-crust cups with the cream cheese filling until the filling reaches the top of the cupcake liners.

13. Bake for 15 to 20 minutes, until the tops begin to brown. Cool completely on a cooling rack.

14. Refrigerate for 1 to 2 hours to firm the cupcakes before serving.

Banana Nut Cheesecake

Don't even start on how you don't like banana-flavored anything. Well, this isn't banana flavored. This is pure banana baked into a creamy cheesecake, bound to turn you into a believer. The added bonus of the nutty crunch makes this all too irresistible.

Makes one 9-inch cheesecake

1 recipe Simple as Pie Crust (page 201), prebaked

2 cups non-hydrogenated vegan cream cheese (recommended: Tofutti), softened

¾ cup plus 2 tablespoons vegan sour cream (recommended: Tofutti)

1 ¼ cups (8.75 ounces) sugar

½ cup (2.5 ounces) all-purpose flour

2 tablespoons egg replacer (recommended: Ener-G)

¾ cup water

1 ripe banana, mashed

2 teaspoons vanilla extract

½ cup almonds, ground

1. Preheat the oven to 350ºF.
2. Line the sides of the prepared springform pan with a 2-inch strip of parchment paper.
3. In the bowl of a stand mixer, mix the cream cheese with the paddle attachment until soft and smooth, about 3 minutes.
4. Add the sour cream and mix to combine.
5. Add the sugar and beat until fluffy, 3 more minutes.
6. Add the flour and mix until smooth.
7. In a small bowl, whisk together the egg replacer and water.
8. Add the egg replacer mixture, banana, vanilla, and almonds to the cream cheese mixture and mix until thoroughly combined.
9. Wrap the bottom of the springform pan with aluminum foil to prevent leaks.

10. Pour the filling into the prepared pie crust.

11. Place the pan inside a deep baking dish that is a few inches larger than the springform pan.

12. Fill the baking dish with enough hot water to reach halfway up the springform pan.

13. Carefully place the pan in the oven and bake for 1 to 1 ½ hours, until the cake rises slightly and begins pulling away from the sides of the pan. The middle should be set.

14. Carefully remove the pan from the water bath and cool completely on a cooling rack.

15. Cover with plastic and refrigerate until completely chilled, at least 8 hours or overnight. Open the springform and remove the strip of parchment before serving.

Pumpkin Cheesecake

D o you see a trend? We love pumpkin and will search any vehicle for its delivery into our pie hole. The spices, the pumpkin, the creamy cheesecake flavor—delectable.

Makes one 9-inch cheesecake

1 recipe Simple as Pie Crust (page 201), prebaked

1 1/2 cups non-hydrogenated vegan cream cheese (recommended: Tofutti), softened

2 1/2 cups canned pumpkin puree (not pumpkin pie filling)

1/2 cup plus 1 tablespoon (4 ounces) sugar

1/3 cup (2.3 ounces) brown sugar

1/4 cup (1.25 ounces) all-purpose flour

2 teaspoons ground cinnamon

1/2 teaspoon ground allspice

1/2 teaspoon ground nutmeg

1/4 teaspoon salt

1 teaspoon lemon juice

1. Preheat the oven to 350°F.
2. Line the sides of the prepared springform pan with a 2-inch strip of parchment paper.
3. In the bowl of a stand mixer, mix the cream cheese with the paddle attachment until soft and smooth, about 3 minutes.
4. Add the pumpkin to the cream cheese and mix until well combined, about 2 more minutes.
5. Add the sugars and mix to combine.
6. Add the flour, cinnamon, allspice, nutmeg, and salt and mix to combine.
7. Add the lemon juice and mix until combined and smooth.
8. Pour the filling into the prepared pie crust and bake for 40 to 50 minutes, until the top is set.

9. Cool completely on a cooling rack.

10. Cover and refrigerate until chilled, at least 8 hours or overnight. Open the springform and remove the strip of parchment before serving.

VARIATION: GINGERSNAP CRUST

Use gingersnaps in place of graham crackers for your crust for extra flair!

Key Lime Cheesecake

This one makes everyone's mouth water here at Sticky Fingers. It hardly makes it to the front case—the staff can't help themselves, and tiny bites turn into desperate mouthfuls.

Makes one 9-inch cheesecake

1 recipe Simple as Pie Crust (page 201), prebaked

3 ½ cups non-hydrogenated vegan cream cheese (recommended: Tofutti), softened

1 cup plus 2 tablespoons (7.9 ounces) sugar

¾ cup (3.75 ounces) all-purpose flour

2 tablespoons egg replacer (recommended: Ener-G)

¾ cup water

1 teaspoon lime zest

½ cup key lime juice, fresh or bottled (recommended: Nellie and Joe's)

1. Preheat the oven to 350°F.
2. Line the sides of the prepared springform pan with a 2-inch strip of parchment paper.
3. In the bowl of a stand mixer, mix the cream cheese with the paddle attachment until soft and smooth, about 3 minutes.
4. Add the sugar and beat until fluffy, 3 more minutes.
5. Add the flour and mix until smooth.
6. In a small bowl, whisk together the egg replacer and water.
7. Add the egg replacer mixture, lime zest, and lime juice to the cream cheese mixture and mix until thoroughly combined.
8. Wrap the bottom of the springform pan with aluminum foil to prevent leaks.
9. Pour the filling into the prepared pie crust. Place the pan inside a deep baking dish that is a few inches larger than the springform pan.

10. Fill the baking dish with enough hot water to reach halfway up the springform pan.

11. Carefully place the pan in the oven and bake for 1 to 1 ½ hours, until the cake rises slightly and begins pulling away from the sides of the pan. The middle will be shiny and not set but will firm up as it cools.

12. Carefully remove the pan from the water bath and cool completely on a cooling rack.

13. Cover and refrigerate the cheesecake until completely chilled, at least 8 hours or overnight. Open the springform and remove the strip of parchment before serving.

Love Bite

Lime

You've never smelled a lime that didn't make your mouth water. You want it so badly, all you have to do is savor the aroma and you salivate. That bittersweet citrus makes you pucker, but in a good way. For me, it's one of those flavors that I can't get enough of. So I don't. I put it on and in everything I can, and then some. I even have lime body lotion. I'm addicted. I read something that said that the juice of two limes per day will help you lose weight, up to two pounds weekly. It didn't say I had to drink it straight, right? Check out this lime cheesecake and let me know if you start losing weight. We may be on to something.

Chocolate Cheesecake

Of course there is a chocolate cheesecake! Would we deny you of such luscious luxury? Heck, no!

Makes one 9-inch cheesecake

1 recipe Simple as Pie Crust (page 201), prebaked

2 ½ cups non-hydrogenated vegan cream cheese (recommended: Tofutti), softened

¾ cup (5.25 ounces) sugar

2 tablespoons egg replacer (recommended: Ener-G)

¾ cup water

2 cups chocolate chips, melted

1 ½ teaspoons vanilla extract

¾ cup coconut creamer (recommended: So Delicious)

1. Preheat the oven to 350ºF.
2. Line the sides of the prepared springform pan with a 2-inch strip of parchment paper.
3. In the bowl of a stand mixer, mix the cream cheese with the paddle attachment until soft and smooth, about 3 minutes.
4. Add the sugar and beat until fluffy, 3 more minutes.
5. In a small bowl, whisk together the egg replacer and water.
6. Add the egg replacer mixture, melted chocolate chips, and vanilla to the cream cheese mixture and mix until thoroughly combined.
7. Add the coconut creamer to the cream cheese mixture and mix until smooth.
8. Wrap the bottom of the springform pan with aluminum foil to prevent leaks.
9. Pour the filling into the prepared pie crust.
10. Place the pan inside a deep baking dish that is a few inches larger than the springform pan. Fill the baking dish with enough hot water to reach halfway up the springform pan.

11. Carefully place the pan in the oven and bake for 1 to 1 ½ hours, until the cake rises slightly and begins pulling away from the sides of the pan. The middle will be shiny and not set but will firm up as it cools.

12. Carefully remove the pan from the water bath and cool completely on a cooling rack.

13. Cover with plastic and refrigerate the cheesecake until completely chilled, at least 8 hours or overnight. Open the springform and remove the strip of parchment before serving.

Chocolate Marble Cheesecake

Marble swirl gets me every time. The dark chocolate burst in each bite is pure chocolaty heaven. And what a looker!

Makes one 9-inch cheesecake

1 recipe Simple as Pie Crust (page 201), prebaked

3 cups non-hydrogenated vegan cream cheese (recommended: Tofutti), softened

1 cup vegan sour cream (recommended: Tofutti)

1 cup plus 2 tablespoons (7.9 ounces) sugar

3 tablespoons egg replacer (recommended: Ener-G)

1 cup water

2 teaspoons vanilla extract

¼ cup (1.25 ounces) all-purpose flour

½ cup melted chocolate (from about 1 cup chocolate chips)

1. Preheat the oven to 350ºF.
2. Line the sides of the prepared springform pan with a 2-inch strip of parchment paper.
3. In the bowl of a stand mixer, mix the cream cheese with the paddle attachment until soft and smooth, about 3 minutes.
4. Add the sour cream and mix to combine.
5. Add the sugar and beat until fluffy, 3 more minutes.
6. In a small bowl, whisk together the egg replacer and water. Add the egg replacer mixture and vanilla to the cream cheese mixture and mix until thoroughly combined.
7. Add the flour and mix until smooth.
8. Remove about two-thirds of the batter to a separate bowl and set aside.

9. Add the melted chocolate to the remaining one-third of the batter and mix until the chocolate is thoroughly incorporated.

10. Scoop out about ½ cup of the chocolate batter and set aside.

11. Wrap the bottom of the springform pan with aluminum foil to prevent leaks.

12. Pour half of the non-chocolate batter into the prepared pie crust.

13. Pour the chocolate batter on top of that.

14. Pour the remaining non-chocolate batter on the very top, so that you have 3 layers of batter in your pan.

15. Take the reserved ½ cup of chocolate batter and drop spoonfuls of it into the pan. Using the tip of a butter knife or a toothpick, randomly drag through the batter to create a swirled, or marbled, effect.

16. Place the pan inside a deep baking dish that is a few inches larger than the springform pan. Fill the baking dish with enough hot water to reach halfway up the springform pan.

17. Carefully place the pan in the oven and bake for 1 to 1 ½ hours, until the cake rises slightly and begins pulling away from the sides of the pan. The middle will be shiny and not set but will firm up as it cools. Carefully remove the pan from the water bath and cool completely on a cooling rack.

18. Cover with plastic and refrigerate until the cheesecake is completely chilled, at least 8 hours or overnight. Open the springform and remove the strip of parchment before serving.

Chocolate Raspberry Cheesecake

I t's not always about what you wear to the party, but what you bring for others to enjoy. This will surely give you the highest props from even the most popular kids. No one can resist the allure of the raspberry and chocolate union.

Makes one 9-inch cheesecake

1 recipe Simple as Pie Crust (page 201), prebaked

1 3/4 cups non-hydrogenated vegan cream cheese (recommended: Tofutti), softened

3/4 cup vegan sour cream (recommended: Tofutti)

2/3 cup (4.6 ounces) cup sugar

2 tablespoons egg replacer (recommended: Ener-G)

3/4 cup water

2 cups chocolate chips, melted

1 teaspoon vanilla extract

1 tablespoon raspberry liqueur

1 1/2 teaspoons almond extract

2 teaspoons lemon zest

1/2 cup fresh raspberries

1. Preheat the oven to 350ºF.
2. Line the sides of the prepared springform pan with a 2-inch strip of parchment paper.
3. In the bowl of a stand mixer, mix the cream cheese with the paddle attachment until soft and smooth, about 3 minutes.
4. Add the sour cream and mix to combine.
5. Add the sugar and beat until fluffy, 3 more minutes.
6. In a small bowl, whisk together the egg replacer and water.
7. Add the egg replacer mixture, melted chocolate chips, vanilla, raspberry liqueur, almond extract, and lemon zest to the cream cheese mixture and mix until thoroughly combined and smooth.

8. Wrap the bottom of the springform pan with aluminum foil to prevent leaks.

9. Pour the filling into the prepared pie crust.

10. Place the pan inside a deep baking dish that is a few inches larger than the springform pan. Fill the baking dish with enough hot water to reach halfway up the springform pan.

11. Carefully place the pan in the oven and bake for 1 to 1 ½ hours, until the cake rises slightly and begins pulling away from the sides of the pan. The middle will be shiny and not set but will firm up as it cools. Carefully remove the pan from the water bath and cool completely on a cooling rack.

12. Cover with plastic and refrigerate the cheesecake until completely chilled, at least 8 hours or overnight. Open the springform and remove the 2-inch strip of parchment.

13. Garnish with the raspberries and serve.

Love Bite

Raspberries

These red berries, a member of the rose family, smell as good as they taste. Taste as much and as often as you like: They contain about one calorie apiece! It practically takes as much energy to eat one as they have in their little berry body. Plus, research published in *Cancer Letters* touts their cancer-warding properties. Metalloproteinase, enzymes we make that are essential for the development and remodeling of tissues, can be detrimental to our health if produced in abnormally high amounts. These enzymes play a significant role in cancer development by providing a mechanism for its invasion and spread. Raspberries have been shown to inhibit metalloproteinase and save the day, saving you from cancer. Will raspberries save both your waistline and your life?

Mint Chocolate Cheesecake

When you indulge in this creamy cheesecake, it will be like the gentle summer air blowing over the chill of the tundra. Move over York, we got this.

Makes one 9-inch cheesecake

1 recipe Simple as Pie Crust (page 201), prebaked

3 cups non-hydrogenated vegan cream cheese (recommended: Tofutti), softened

⅓ cup vegan sour cream (recommended: Tofutti)

¾ cup (5.25 ounces) sugar

1 ½ tablespoons egg replacer (recommended: Ener-G)

½ cup water

2 teaspoons vanilla extract

1 cup chocolate chips, melted

1 teaspoon peppermint extract

1. Preheat the oven to 350ºF.
2. Line the sides of the prepared springform pan with a 2-inch strip of parchment paper.
3. In the bowl of a stand mixer, mix the cream cheese with the paddle attachment until soft and smooth, about 3 minutes.
4. Add the sour cream to the cream cheese and mix to combine.
5. Add the sugar and beat until fluffy, 3 more minutes.
6. In a small bowl, whisk together the egg replacer and water.
7. Add the egg replacer mixture, vanilla, melted chocolate chips, and peppermint extract to the cream cheese mixture and mix until thoroughly combined.
8. Wrap the bottom of the springform pan with aluminum foil to prevent leaks.
9. Pour the filling into the prepared pie crust.
10. Place the pan inside a deep baking dish that is a few inches larger than the

springform pan. Fill the baking dish with enough hot water to reach halfway up the springform pan.

11. Carefully place the pan in the oven and bake for about 1 hour, until the cake rises slightly and begins pulling away from the sides of the pan. The middle will be shiny and not set. It will continue to bake and set as it rests.

12. Carefully remove the pan from the water bath and cool completely on a cooling rack.

13. Cover and refrigerate the cheesecake until completely chilled, at least 8 hours or overnight. Open the springform and remove the strip of parchment before serving.

Mocha Chocolate Cheesecake

We can't stay away from the mocha-licious combo. So rich and satisfying, we couldn't deny a cheesecake of this magnificent mix. Paired together in this creamy cheesecake is just, well, dreamy.

Makes one 9-inch cheesecake

1 recipe Simple as Pie Crust (page 201), prebaked

3 cups non-hydrogenated vegan cream cheese (recommended: Tofutti), softened

1 cup plus 2 tablespoons (7.9 ounces) sugar

1 ½ tablespoons egg replacer (recommended: Ener-G)

¾ cup water

¾ cup chocolate chips, melted

¾ cup (3.75 ounces) all-purpose flour

3 tablespoons rum

3 ½ tablespoons instant coffee powder

1 ½ teaspoons vanilla extract

1. Preheat the oven to 350°F.
2. Line the sides of the prepared springform pan with a 2-inch strip of parchment paper.
3. In the bowl of a stand mixer, mix the cream cheese with the paddle attachment until soft and smooth, about 3 minutes.
4. Add the sugar and beat until fluffy, 3 more minutes.
5. In a small bowl, whisk together the egg replacer and ½ cup of the water.
6. Add the egg replacer mixture, melted chocolate chips, and flour to the cream cheese mixture and mix until thoroughly combined.
7. In a small bowl, mix together the rum, coffee granules, remaining ¼ cup

water, and the vanilla. Add the coffee mixture to the cream cheese mixture and mix until smooth.

8. Wrap the bottom of the springform pan with aluminum foil to prevent leaks.

9. Pour the filling into the prepared pie crust.

10. Place the pan inside a deep baking dish that is a few inches larger than the springform pan. Fill the baking dish with enough hot water to reach halfway up the springform pan.

11. Carefully place the pan in the oven and bake for 1 to 1 1/2 hours, until the cake rises slightly and begins pulling away from the sides of the pan. The middle will be shiny and not set. It will continue to bake and set as it rests.

12. Carefully remove the pan from the water bath and cool completely on a cooling rack.

13. Cover with plastic and refrigerate the cheesecake until completely chilled, at least 8 hours or overnight. Open the springform and remove the strip of parchment before serving.

Cream Pies

Who doesn't love cream pies? The slightly sweet crust with smooth filling covered with your favorite topper? Ever try sliced fruit, ice cream (our favorite is the coconut milk ice creams), or whipped crème (we love the easy bases by Soyatoo or MimicCreme!)? The thought just makes me swoon! If there is one thing I can convince you of, it's to eat the pie in its total form—please resist the temptation of eating the filling before you fill the pie shell. The enjoyment factor will be tenfold compared to individualized eating, promise.

Vanilla Cream Pie

Think of this as your "cream pie how-to." Learn this one and you are good to go.

Makes one 9-inch pie

1 recipe Simple as Pie Crust
   (page 201)
2 cups soymilk
3 tablespoons cornstarch
½ cup (3.5 ounces) sugar

¼ teaspoon salt
1 teaspoon vanilla extract
1 tablespoon non-hydrogenated
   vegan margarine (recommended:
   Earth Balance)

1. Preheat the oven to 350°F.
2. Lightly grease a 9-inch pie pan that's at least 1 ½ inches deep.
3. Roll the pie dough out to a 13-inch circle and fit it into the pan. Crimp the edges above the rim.
4. Bake for 15 minutes, then cool completely while you make the pie filling.
5. In a small bowl, whisk together ¼ cup of the soymilk with the cornstarch to make a slurry. Set aside.
6. In a medium heavy-bottomed saucepan, combine the remaining 1 ¾ cups soymilk, the sugar, and salt and heat until bubbles begin to form at the edges.
7. Slowly whisk in the cornstarch slurry and cook, whisking, for 1 to 2 minutes, until the mixture thickens enough to coat the back of a metal spoon. Do not bring to a full boil.
8. Remove from the heat and stir in the vanilla and margarine. Strain the cooked pie filling through a fine-mesh sieve to remove any lumps before pouring it into your pie crust.
9. Pour into the prepared pie crust, cover with plastic, and chill 2 to 4 hours until firm.

Lemon Cream Pie

This is the dream that pies were made from. Light and fluffy clouds of pure lemon love. It will make you purse your lips for more.

Makes one 9-inch pie

1 recipe Simple as Pie Crust
   (page 201)
2 cups lemon juice
1 cup (7 ounces) sugar
¼ cup water

2 tablespoons egg replacer
   (recommended: Ener-G)
6 tablespoons silken tofu
3 ½ tablespoons cornstarch

1. Preheat the oven to 350°F.
2. Lightly grease a 9-inch pie pan that's at least 1 ½ inches deep.
3. Roll the pie dough out to a 13-inch circle and fit it into the pan. Crimp the edges above the rim.
4. Bake for 15 minutes, then set aside to cool completely while you make the pie filling.
5. In a medium heavy-bottomed saucepan, heat the lemon juice and ½ cup of the sugar over medium heat and stir until the sugar dissolves.
6. In a blender or food processor, combine the water, egg replacer, tofu, cornstarch, and the remaining ½ cup sugar and puree until smooth.
7. Add the tofu mixture to the saucepan with the hot lemon juice and bring to a boil.
8. Cook, whisking, until the mixture is very thick, about 5 minutes. If necessary, pour the cooked pie filling through a fine-mesh sieve to remove any lumps before pouring it into your pie crust.
9. Pour into the prepared pie crust, cover with plastic, and refrigerate for 2 to 4 hours, until firm.

Love Bite

....

Cornstarch

I know what you are thinking. How can cornstarch have any redeeming qualities other than making gravy and that weird quicksand that you can walk on? Well, I'm here to tell you that there is one amazing quality to cornstarch like no other. It's not so much what it is but rather what it is not: Cornstarch gelatinizes when cooked with liquid and will set when cooled. That means we can have puddings, fillings, and curds that stand up on their own but need no eggs or gelatin to do so. Lucky for us, the taste is virtually nonexistent, which leaves us in control of flavor making.

Coconut Crème Pie

This crème of the crop can do no wrong, as it is perfect regardless of how you enjoy it. Top this little lovely with extra toasted coconut or your favorite fresh fruit. Drizzle chocolate and add nuts for a candy bar look-alike (and taste-alike). Or simply enjoy as is and devour as soon as it's ready.

Makes one 9-inch pie

1 recipe Simple as Pie Crust
   (page 201)
2 cups coconut milk (recommended:
   So Delicious)
3 tablespoons cornstarch
½ cup (3.5 ounces) sugar

¼ teaspoon salt
1 cup toasted flaked coconut
1 teaspoon vanilla extract
1 tablespoon non-hydrogenated
   vegan margarine (recommended:
   Earth Balance)

1. Preheat the oven to 350°F.
2. Toast the coconut: Spread shredded coconut in a thin layer on a baking sheet. Bake for 5 to 7 minutes, until it begins to brown. Stir and bake for an additional 2 to 4 minutes, until it toasts evenly. Set aside.
3. Lightly grease a 9-inch pie pan that's at least 1 ½ inches deep.
4. Roll the pie dough out to a 13-inch circle and fit it into the pan. Crimp the edges above the rim.
5. Bake for 15 minutes, then set aside to cool completely while you make the pie filling.
6. In a small bowl, whisk together ¼ cup of the coconut milk with the cornstarch to make a slurry. Set aside.
7. In a medium, heavy-bottomed saucepan, combine the remaining 1 ¾ cups coconut milk, the sugar, and salt and heat until bubbles begin to form at the edges.
8. Slowly whisk in the cornstarch slurry and cook, whisking, for 1 to 2 minutes,

until the mixture thickens enough to coat the back of a metal spoon. Do not bring to a full boil.

9. Remove from the heat and stir in the tosted coconut, vanilla, and margarine.

10. Pour into the prepared pie crust, cover with plastic, and refrigerate for 2 to 4 hours, until firm.

Love Bite

Coconut

Function and fashion? Nutritious and delicious? The health benefits of coconut are endless. From hair tonic to cholesterol reducer, antiviral properties to soap making, the coconut is multifaceted and multidelicious. You can use the fat to cook with just about anything; the meat can be enjoyed fresh, dried, or dried and toasted; the water contains the minerals you need to help keep you hydrated; and the milk, made from extracting the liquid and fat from the meat, is the closest we've ever come to the nectar of the gods.

Key Lime Pie

Can you hear it? Can you hear the sounds of the ocean, feel the warm breeze, and enjoy the sweet-tart taste of Key West's claim to fame?

Makes one 9-inch pie

1 recipe Simple as Pie Crust
(page 201)
1 ½ tablespoons cornstarch
½ cup key lime juice, fresh or
bottled (recommended: Nellie
and Joe's)

2 cups non-hydrogenated vegan
cream cheese (recommended:
Tofutti), softened
1 cup (7 ounces) sugar
1 ½ teaspoons vanilla extract

1. Preheat the oven to 350°F.
2. Lightly grease a 9-inch pie pan that's at least 1 ½ inches deep.
3. Roll the pie dough out to a 13-inch circle and fit it into the pan. Crimp the edges above the rim.
4. Bake for 15 minutes, then set aside to cool completely while you make the pie filling.
5. In a small, heavy-bottomed saucepan, dissolve the cornstarch in the lime juice over medium heat.
6. Bring to a boil, stirring constantly.
7. Reduce the heat and simmer until the mixture begins to thicken, about 2 minutes.
8. Remove from the heat and set aside to cool.
9. In the bowl of a stand mixer, mix the cream cheese with the paddle attachment until soft and smooth, about 3 minutes.
10. Add the sugar, and cream together until smooth and fluffy, about 3 more minutes.

11. Add the thickened lime juice mixture and the vanilla to the cream cheese mixture and mix until combined and smooth.

12. Pour the filling into the prepared pie crust, cover with plastic, and refrigerate for at least 2 hours before serving.

Love Bite

Key Lime

If the key lime is anything at all, it is freaking cute. And it's freakishly strong, packed with more health benefits and flavor than its relatively giant counterparts. Vitamin C, potassium, flavanoids, and folic acid, to name a few or four, make this little fruit a giant in the healthy foods department. No, don't be scared! It's like a delicious flavor-filled candy dressed up to look like a fruit. Embrace the taste.

Fruit Tart

Fruit tarts are delightful for any occasion. And beautiful! An edible centerpiece if you ask me. We use pastry crème for the crème part, but you can use any filling, curd, or pudding you like. How do they make those tarts so perfect and shiny at the store? Brushing with apricot glaze is an easy and tasty way to preserve and present cut fruit. The citric acid from the apricots helps keep the color, and the sugar glaze protects it from drying out.

Makes one 9-inch tart

1 recipe Simple as Pie Crust (page 201)
1 recipe Pastry Crème (page 57)
3 cups of your favorite fruit—fresh berries of your choice (such as raspberries, blueberries, or sliced strawberries) or sliced kiwi
Apricot preserves, for glaze

1. Preheat the oven to 350°F.
2. Lightly grease a 9-inch tart pan with a removable bottom.
3. Roll the pie dough out to a 13-inch circle and fit it into the pan. Press the dough evenly into the bottom and up the sides of the tart pan.
4. Bake for 15 minutes, then set aside to cool completely.
5. Scoop the prepared pastry crème into the prepared pie crust.
6. Decoratively place the fruit on top of the tart to cover the pastry crème, cover with plastic, and chill for at least 2 hours before serving.
7. To glaze: Melt apricot preserves in the top part of a double boiler or in a microwave, making sure they are smooth and lump-free.
8. Grab a pastry brush and lightly brush the fruit with the glaze. Be generous.
9. Refrigerate to set and serve.

HINT

If you think you might have the willpower to leave some tart for tomorrow's dessert, you may want to prep your crust for an extra day of sitting before pouring in your filling. Brush your crust with melted chocolate and allow it to set for 5 to 10 minutes before adding your crème. This will help keep your crust light and crisp rather than heavy and soggy.

Chocolate Cream Pie

If you miss that fun pudding flavor, that delicious treat Bill Cosby brought to fame in the eighties, then do I have a treat for you. Super simple and extremely tasty, and so equal opportunity: You can enjoy when it's warm or wait till it's chilled.

Makes one 9-inch pie

1 recipe Simple as Pie Crust
   (page 201)
2 cups soymilk
3 tablespoons cornstarch
½ cup (3.5 ounces) sugar

⅓ cup (1.25 ounces) cocoa powder
   (see Note)
¼ teaspoon salt
1 teaspoon vanilla extract

1. Preheat the oven to 350°F.
2. Lightly grease a 9-inch pie pan that's at least 1 ½ inches deep.
3. Roll the pie dough out to a 13-inch circle and set it into the pan. Crimp the edges above the rim.
4. Bake for 15 minutes, then set aside to cool completely while you make the pie filling.
5. In a small bowl, whisk together ¼ cup of the soymilk with the cornstarch to make a slurry. Set aside.
6. In a medium, heavy-bottomed saucepan, whisk together the sugar, cocoa powder, and salt.
7. Add the remaining 1 ¾ cups soymilk and heat until bubbles begin to form at the edges.
8. Slowly whisk in the cornstarch slurry and cook, whisking, for 1 to 2 minutes, until the mixture thickens enough to coat the back of a metal spoon. Do not bring to a full boil.
9. Remove from the heat and stir in the vanilla. If necessary, pour the cooked

this is warm choc pudding

pie filling through a fine-mesh sieve to remove any lumps before pouring it into your pie crust.

10. Pour the filling into the prepared pie crust, cover with plastic, and chill 2 to 4 hours, until firm.

NOTE

If you prefer a richer filling, replace the cocoa powder with 6 ounces of finely chopped good-quality dark chocolate (60% or higher). Add the chocolate to the filling just before adding the vanilla and stir until it is smooth and creamy.

Peanut Butter Pie

You have to wake up early to be a baker, and our morning baker Kevin can tell you all about it. He gets everything ready for the bakery case and makes sure we have backup, from cookies to frosting. You have to really enjoy a routine and appreciate repetition to be a morning baker. But everyone has their moments. One day, I came in to find Kevin whipping up these little sweetie pies, which are now part of Kevin's daily duties.

Makes one 9-inch pie

1 recipe Simple as Pie Crust
    (page 201), prebaked
1 ½ pounds firm tofu (do not use
    silken)
1 ½ cups smooth peanut butter
    (recommended: Skippy
    Natural)

1 cup plus 2 tablespoons
    (7.9 ounces) sugar
1 ½ tablespoons vanilla
    extract
½ cup chocolate chips, melted
    (optional)

1. Line the sides of the prepared springform pan with a 2-inch strip of parchment paper.
2. In a blender, combine the tofu, peanut butter, sugar, and vanilla and blend until smooth.
3. Pour the mixture into the prepared pie crust, cover with plastic, and chill for at least 8 hours, until firm.
4. Open the springform and remove the strip of parchment before serving.
5. Drizzle melted chocolate across the top of the pie, if you like.

ADDED BONUS: BROWNIE CRUST!

Have you made the brownie recipe yet (page 178)? Do you have any left over? If you do, you can take a couple, crumble them up, and press them into a pie pan to use as a crust. Trust me, it's not a brownie sacrifice. It's like the brownie is giving back to the bakery community. We do it, and it's worth every mouthful.

Chapter 10

We've Got Seoul

True story: My longtime bud and helper of all things Sticky Fingers happens to be Korean American. Born here in this country (her parents are from back East), she has a true appreciation for all things Korean, and all sweets American. So it was no surprise when she offered to help us make our first round of brochures and business cards, for free, or rather for a small trade in treats. She happens to also be a kick-ass compassionate protector of all animals. So when KBS, the South Korean version of our CBS, wanted to include her life and work on an hour-long episode of a KBS weekly documentary series, a 60 Minutes-style show, she shyly agreed. Camera crews followed her around, chatting up family and friends, and kept a close eye on her daily doings. She came into our little basement shop to introduce the crew to vegan baking (and to get her own fix, I'm sure), and suddenly the cameras were on us. When the show aired, turns out we had a couple of seconds of fame on my bestie's show. So proud of her and kind of excited for ourselves, we didn't think much more about it.

A few weeks later we began getting lovely e-mails from a very sweet man hailing from Seoul, South Korea, who wanted to bring his friend to see our shop. Not only had they seen us on the KBS show, they had tasted our treats while visiting family here in DC and were blown away by the vegan concept. Health, he explained, was very important to many Koreans. Food grown and manufactured in South Korea often is both non-GMO and organic by our standards. Cholesterol-free would be a great draw, as would the low-cal and fat-free options. We quickly corrected him, explaining the nutrient facts and calorie reality of our goods, and we thought that would be the end of it. But it wasn't. They were determined to bring Sticky Fingers to Seoul. We weren't so sure.

"We can't do this," one of us said, choking. "How can we get everything together? We have no idea what we are doing. They have their MBAs; we don't have professional business degrees. They will see right through us and kill the entire deal!"

So we said yes.

We took a good long look at how and what we were doing here, and we wrote it all down. We put together a training manual, a book of all of our recipes and techniques, and any other info they wanted to include. They visited stateside for three weeks to work with us in our kitchen and to learn how to bake vegan-style firsthand. They watched us closely to see how we worked our magic with the utensils, tools, and equipment in our bakeshop.

Then it was our turn. Head baker Ben (now general manager) and I headed to Korea for almost three weeks for an amazing opportunity to work with them in their kitchen. It was fantastic and a lot like, well, working in a bakery in the middle of Seoul. It was work, but it was so much fun. We stayed at the Sunshine Hotel, blocks away from the sparkly and new Sticky Fingers Bakery Seoul. The first time I saw the sign above the door, I cried. The first time I saw their super-fancy packaging, I cried. The first time I saw their sticky buns, I cried. It's surprising I could get any work done with all those tears in my eyes!

They opened their first store at eleven a.m. on November 11, 2005. There was a huge turnout from the people who made the first international Sticky Fingers happen, and then some. A spread of all their cookies was laid out proudly before us by team Sticky-Seoul. It was a day I will never forget. And every year the original manager sends me a warm and sentimental anniversary e-mail. Cute!

Now they boast a main store with (so far) eight other kiosk locations in high-end gourmet emporiums—think the makeup counters in department stores but with food instead. We've included some of their best-selling recipes and our favorites in the pages that follow. Every year they send us one of their holiday combo packs filled with mini pound cakes, wrapped and dressed in ribbon. Cookies, too, in heart-shaped plastic containers sealed closed with Sticky Fingers stickers. All nestled into the most perfect boxes made to carry each container perfectly and safely to its eagerly awaiting recipient. Neatly tied in a bow and boasting our logo and name. Exquisite. The attention to detail is something I have yet to witness anywhere else, and is something we strive for.

It's interesting what you learn from those you attempt to teach. We went in thinking we were simply licensing the rights to a group in Korea. But what we got out of it was ten times that. We held a mirror up to ourselves, which forced us to take the business and the recipes to the next level. We learned that we weren't just a little vegan bakery hiding in DC, and we were no longer just one store. The knowledge and confidence we gained through the experience was overpowering. We returned home ready for more and hungry for the next adventure. Soon after, we planned our expansion and move from the tiny little basement location hidden under a flight of stairs in Dupont Circle to the up and coming, bustling, and much bigger area of Columbia Heights. We found our voice, our true mission, and the courage to become bigger, bolder, and better. We were proud. Amazing what life brings to you when you simply follow your heart.

Seoul Sticky Bread

I love getting recipes from our sister store in Korea, especially when they take one of our recipes and turn it into their own. They do everything with this, dozens of variations, such as sprinkling with sesame seeds, adding currants to the batter, or enjoying as toast with jam.

Makes 4 loaves

1 tablespoon active dry yeast

1 ¾ cups warm water

½ cup (3.5 ounces) sugar

1 tablespoon salt

1 ¼ cups soymilk, at room temperature

⅓ cup non-hydrogenated vegan margarine (recommended: Earth Balance)

7 cups (2 pounds, 3 ounces) all-purpose flour

1. In a bowl, combine the yeast, water, and ¼ cup of the sugar. Set aside until the mixture begins to bubble and doubles in size, 15 to 20 minutes.
2. In a large bowl, combine the remaining ¼ cup sugar and the salt. Cut in the margarine until you have medium crumbs. Stir in the soymilk.
3. Add the yeast mixture to the margarine mixture and stir until combined.
4. Slowly add in 6 cups of the flour until all the flour is incorporated; you can do this with a wooden spoon or by hand. The dough should be slightly sticky and soft, not firm.
5. Let the dough stand in the bowl and cover with a damp dishtowel in a warm area of the room until it doubles in size, about 1 hour.
6. Preheat the oven to 350°F.
7. Grease and flour 4 loaf (9 by 5-inch, or 1-pound) pans and set aside.
8. Once the dough has doubled in size, hand-knead the dough while sprinkling in the remaining 1 cup flour on your work surface and dough to help avoid sticking, until the dough is firm.

9. Divide the dough into 4 pieces and form them into balls, tucking the corners so you have a smooth top.

10. Place each dough ball into a loaf pan.

11. Using a sharp knife or a razor blade, make 3 slits in the top of each loaf. This will allow the loaves to expand while baking.

12. Bake for 40 minutes, or until the bread springs back when you press it with a finger.

13. Cool completely on a cooling rack.

14. Use a dough scraper or plastic spatula to loosen the loaves away from the edges before turning them out of the pans.

Seoul Mocha Bread

This is what I'm talking about! Take the basics and come up with your own renditions of our favorite recipes. This is a twist on our sticky bun recipe (page 116), so you totally know how to do this one. The addition of raisins is surprisingly tasty up against the coffee flavor. Very nice work, Team Sticky-Seoul!

Makes 2 loaves

1 tablespoon active dry yeast

½ cup warm water

⅓ cup plus 1 ½ tablespoons (2.8 ounces) sugar

1 tablespoon instant coffee powder

1 ½ teaspoons salt

⅔ cup soymilk, at room temperature

⅓ cup non-hydrogenated vegan margarine (recommended: Earth Balance)

½ cup raisins

⅔ cup walnuts, chopped

3 ½ cups (1 pound, 1.5 ounces) all-purpose flour

1. In a bowl, combine the yeast, water, and ¼ cup of the sugar. Set aside until the mixture begins to bubble and doubles in size, 15 to 20 minutes.
2. In a large bowl, combine the remaining sugar, coffee, and the salt. Cut in the margarine until you have medium-sized crumbs. Stir in the soymilk.
3. Add the yeast mixture to the margarine mixture and stir together until combined.
4. Stir in the raisins and walnuts.
5. Slowly add 3 cups of the flour until all of the flour is incorporated; you can do this with a wooden spoon or by hand. The dough should be slightly sticky and soft rather than firm.
6. Let the dough stand in the bowl with a damp dishtowel in a warm area of the room until it doubles in size, about 1 hour.
7. Preheat the oven to 350ºF.

8. Grease and flour 2 loaf (9 by 5-inch, or 1-pound) pans and set aside.

9. Once the dough has doubled in size, hand-knead the dough while sprinkling in the remaining ½ cup flour on your work surface and dough to help avoid sticking, until the dough is firm.

10. Divide the dough in half and form into balls, tucking the corners so you have a smooth top.

11. Place each dough ball into a loaf pan.

12. Using a sharp knife or a razor blade, make 3 slits in the top of each loaf. This will allow the loaves to expand while baking.

13. Bake for 40 minutes, or until the dough springs back when you press it with a finger.

14. Cool completely on a cooling rack.

15. Use a dough scraper or plastic spatula to loosen the loaves away from the edges before turning them out of the pans.

Seoul Nutty Pound Cake

Traditional pound cakes were simply a pound of butter, a pound of flour, a pound of eggs, and a pound of sugar. Obviously that wouldn't work for us. Here is our sister store's reincarnation of an old-time favorite.

Makes 2 large loaves or 8 mini loaves

1 cup non-hydrogenated vegan margarine (recommended: Earth Balance)

2 ½ cups (1 pound, 1.5 ounces) sugar

2 teaspoons egg replacer (recommended: Ener-G)

1 cup plus 2 tablespoons water

4 ¾ cups plus 1 ½ tablespoons (1 pound, 8 ounces) all-purpose flour

2/3 cup plus 1 tablespoon (2.8 ounces) almond flour

1 tablespoon baking powder

½ teaspoon salt

½ cup walnuts, chopped

½ cup toasted chestnuts (see Note)

1 cup plus 2 tablespoons soymilk

3 tablespoons vegetable or canola oil

1 tablespoon almond extract

1. Preheat the oven to 350°F.
2. Grease and flour 2 loaf (9 by 5-inch, or 1-pound) pans or 8 mini loaf pans and set aside.
3. In the bowl of a stand mixer, combine the margarine and sugar, and cream with the paddle attachment until light and fluffy, 2 to 3 minutes. Scrape the bottom of the bowl to ensure that the ingredients are combined and mix for 30 seconds more.
4. In a small bowl, whisk together the egg replacer and water. Add to the sugar mixture and mix until everything is well combined.
5. In a large bowl, combine the all-purpose flour, almond flour, baking powder, and salt. Stir in the walnuts and chestnuts.

6. In a separate bowl, combine the soymilk, oil, and almond extract.

7. With the mixer on low (or by hand), slowly add the dry ingredients and soymilk mixture to the sugar mixture, alternating between the two and ending with the soymilk mixture. You will only need a few folds to incorporate. We don't want to lose those bubbles!

8. Scoop the batter evenly into the prepared pans. Smooth the tops gently so there are no peaks to burn.

9. Bake until a toothpick inserted into the center of a loaf comes out clean, 30 to 35 minutes for large loaves, 10 to 15 minutes for mini loaves.

10. Cool completely on a cooling rack.

NOTE

You can toast your own chestnuts for 45 minutes at 400ºF, or you can purchase roasted chestnuts at most international markets (or online, if you're stumped).

Seoul Coffee Pound Cake

Rarely will you find a sugar-laden, overly sweet treat in Seoul. This beauty fits in just right; not too sweet, with a nice bite from the coffee.

Makes 2 large loaves or 8 mini loaves

1 cup plus 2 tablespoons non-hydrogenated vegan margarine (recommended: Earth Balance)

1 1/2 cups plus 2 tablespoons (11.5 ounces) sugar

1 tablespoon egg replacer (recommended: Ener-G)

1/3 cup water

4 1/4 cups (1 pound, 5.2 ounces) all-purpose flour

1 1/2 teaspoons baking powder

1/4 teaspoon salt

3/4 cup walnuts, chopped or halved

3/4 cup plus 1 tablespoon soymilk

2 1/2 tablespoons vegetable or canola oil

1 tablespoon instant espresso powder (or 2 tablespoons instant coffee powder)

1. Preheat the oven to 350ºF.
2. Grease and flour 2 loaf (9 by 5-inch, or 1-pound) pans or 8 mini loaf pans and set aside.
3. In the bowl of a stand mixer, combine the margarine and sugar, and cream with the paddle attachment until light and fluffy, 2 to 3 minutes. Scrape the bottom of the bowl to ensure that the ingredients are combined and mix for 30 seconds more.
4. In a small bowl, whisk together the egg replacer and water. Add to the sugar mixture and mix until everything is well combined.
5. In a large bowl, combine the flour, baking powder, and salt. Stir in the walnuts.
6. In a separate bowl, combine the soymilk, oil, and instant espresso or coffee powder.

7. With the mixer on low (or by hand), slowly add the dry ingredients and soymilk mixture to the sugar mixture, alternating between the two and ending with the soymilk mixture. You will only need a few folds to incorporate. We don't want to lose those bubbles!

8. Scoop the batter evenly into the prepared pans. Smooth the tops gently so there are no peaks to burn.

9. Bake until a toothpick inserted into the center of a loaf comes out clean, 30 to 35 minutes for large loaves, 10 to 15 minutes for mini loaves.

10. Cool completely on a cooling rack.

Seoul Chocolate Pound Cake

So chocolaty good! Not quite cake, but not quite bread, this is a pure mouth pleaser.

Makes 2 large loaves or 8 mini loaves

1 cup plus 2 tablespoons non-hydrogenated vegan margarine (recommended: Earth Balance)

1 1/2 cups plus 2 tablespoons (11.5 ounces) sugar

1 tablespoon egg replacer (recommended: Ener-G)

1/3 cup water

3 3/4 cups plus 3 tablespoons (1 pound, 3.6 ounces) all-purpose flour

1 1/2 teaspoons baking powder

1/2 teaspoon baking soda

1/4 teaspoon salt

1/4 cup (1 ounce) cocoa powder

1/2 cup chocolate chips

3/4 cup plus 1 tablespoon soymilk

2 1/2 tablespoons vegetable or canola oil

1. Preheat the oven to 350ºF.
2. Grease and flour 2 loaf (9 by 5-inch, or 1-pound) pans or 8 mini loaf pans and set aside.
3. In the bowl of a stand mixer, combine the margarine and sugar, and cream with the paddle attachment until light and fluffy, 2 to 3 minutes. Scrape the bottom of the bowl to ensure that the ingredients are combined and mix for 30 seconds more.
4. In a small bowl, whisk together the egg replacer and water. Add to the sugar mixture and mix until everything is well combined.

5. In a large bowl, combine the flour, baking powder, baking soda, salt, and cocoa powder. Stir in the chocolate chips.

6. In a separate bowl, combine the soymilk and oil.

7. With the mixer on low (or by hand), slowly add the dry ingredients and the soymilk mixture to the sugar mixture, alternating between the two and ending with the soymilk mixture. You only need a few folds to incorporate. We don't want to lose those bubbles!

8. Scoop the batter evenly into the prepared pans. Smooth the tops gently so there are no peaks to burn.

9. Bake until a toothpick inserted into the center of a loaf comes out clean, 30 to 35 minutes for large loaves, 10 to 15 minutes for mini loaves.

10. Cool completely on a cooling rack.

Seoul Green Tea Pound Cake

It never dawned on me to put green tea in anything other than hot water or soymilk. Maybe in a face mask, but that was it. Matcha, the young and vibrant green leaf, is ground to a powder as fine as cocoa, making it easy to use in any dessert. The flavor is much "greener" and earthier than plain old green tea bags, and a bit sweeter. It originates in Asia, so it made perfect sense when I opened our holiday package from our Seoul sister store and saw an adorable, rich, green mini pound cake. I bit into it as soon as I could get the wrapper off (lying—I just worked my teeth around it) and was in awe of what I tasted. Have you ever had a green tea latte? That's exactly what it reminded me of, and I enjoyed every morsel.

Makes 2 large loaves or 8 mini loaves

1 cup plus 2 tablespoons non-hydrogenated vegan margarine (recommended: Earth Balance)

1 1/2 cups plus 2 tablespoons (11.5 ounces) sugar

1 tablespoon egg replacer (recommended: Ener-G)

1/3 cup water

4 1/4 cups (1 pound, 5.2 ounces) all-purpose flour

1 1/2 teaspoons baking powder

1/4 teaspoon salt

1 tablespoon green tea (matcha) powder

3/4 cup plus 1 tablespoon soymilk

2 1/2 tablespoons vegetable or canola oil

1 1/2 tablespoons maple syrup

1. Preheat the oven to 350ºF.
2. Grease and flour 2 loaf (9 by 5-inch, or 1-pound) pans or 8 mini loaf pans and set aside.
3. In the bowl of a stand mixer, combine the margarine and sugar, and cream

together with the paddle attachment until light and fluffy, 2 to 3 minutes. Scrape the bottom of the bowl to ensure that the ingredients are combined and mix for 30 seconds more.

4. In a small bowl, whisk together the egg replacer and water. Add to the sugar mixture and mix until everything is well combined.

5. In a large bowl, combine the flour, baking powder, salt, and green tea powder.

6. In a separate bowl, combine the soymilk, oil, and maple syrup.

7. With the mixer on low (or by hand), slowly add the dry ingredients and the soymilk mixture to the sugar mixture, alternating between the two and ending with the soymilk mixture. You only need a few folds to incorporate. We don't want to lose those bubbles!

8. Scoop the batter evenly into the prepared pans. Smooth the tops gently so there are no peaks to burn.

9. Bake until a toothpick inserted into the center of a loaf comes out clean, 30 to 35 minutes for large loaves, 10 to 15 minutes for mini loaves.

10. Cool completely on a cooling rack.

Love Bite

Green Tea

Polyphenols and catechols boast tons of antioxidant power in this little leaf. And the benefits are plenty: reduced risk for pancreatic, lung, stomach, breast, and esophageal cancer; lowered "bad" cholesterol; and support for fat oxidation, causing fat to be broken down rather than stored. You want to reap the amazing benefits, but it can be difficult to drink enough to do so: Who has the time to slug back tea all day? By any means necessary is our motto, so enjoy this pound cake in lieu of a cup or two!

Seoul Walnut Cake

This cake is very light and slightly sweet. Perfect for a coffee or tea break. Or just because.

Makes one 9-inch round cake

2 cups (10 ounces) all-purpose flour

1 1/4 cups (5 ounces) almond flour

2 teaspoons baking powder

1/2 teaspoon salt

1 1/2 cups finely chopped walnuts

1 1/2 cups (10.5 ounces) sugar

3/4 cup non-hydrogenated vegan margarine (recommended: Earth Balance)

1 1/2 teaspoons egg replacer (recommended: Ener-G)

1/3 cup water

1/3 cup soymilk

2 teaspoons vanilla extract

1 teaspoon almond extract

1. Preheat the oven to 350°F.
2. Line a 9-inch round cake pan with parchment paper.
3. Whisk the flours, baking powder, and salt into a medium bowl. Add the walnuts and set the bowl aside.
4. In the bowl of an electric stand mixer, combine the sugar and the margarine, and cream together with the paddle attachment, about 5 minutes. Scrape down the sides and bottom of the bowl.
5. In a small bowl or cup, combine the egg replacer and water and stir to dissolve the egg replacer. Add the egg replacer mixture to the sugar mixture and mix until combined.
6. In a small bowl, combine the soymilk and vanilla and almond extracts.
7. Turn the mixer speed to low and slowly add the dry ingredients and the soymilk mixture, alternating between the two and ending with the soymilk.

8. Spoon the batter evenly into the pan. Bake for 18 to 25 minutes, until a toothpick inserted in the center comes out clean or the cake springs back to the touch.

9. Place the pan on a cooling rack to cool completely, then run a knife or plastic dough scraper around the edges of the pan to loosen the cakes from the sides. Turn the pan upside down to remove the cake.

Seoul Almond Crème Walnut Tart

From what I hear, this is one of the best sellers at the Seoul locations. Stunning!

Makes one 9-inch tart

FOR THE CRUST

2 cups (10 ounces) whole wheat pastry flour

2/3 cup (4.6 ounces) sugar

1/4 teaspoon salt

1/4 teaspoon baking powder

2/3 cup non-hydrogenated vegan margarine (recommended: Earth Balance), chilled and cut into 1/4-inch pieces

FOR THE ALMOND CREAM FILLING

2/3 cup non-hydrogenated vegan margarine (recommended: Earth Balance)

1 cup (7 ounces) sugar

1/2 cup soymilk

2 1/2 tablespoons water

1 tablespoon egg replacer (recommended: Ener-G)

2 cups plus 2 tablespoons (8.5 ounces) almond flour

2 cups (10 ounces) whole wheat pastry flour

1/2 cup walnuts, finely chopped

1. Make the crust: Whisk together the flour, sugar, salt, and baking powder.
2. Cut in the margarine until the mixture is crumbly.
3. Lightly grease a 9-inch tart pan that's at least 1 1/2 inches deep.
4. Roll the tart dough out to a 13-inch circle and fit it into the tart pan. Press the dough evenly into the bottom and along the sides of the pan and crimp the edges above the rim. Refrigerate the crust while you make the filling.

5. Preheat the oven to 350ºF.

6. Make the filling: In the bowl of a stand mixer, combine the margarine and sugar and cream together with the paddle attachment until light and fluffy, about 3 minutes.

7. In a small bowl, combine the soymilk, water, and egg replacer and stir to combine. Add to the sugar mixture and mix until all the ingredients come together.

8. Add the almond flour, whole wheat flour, and walnuts and mix until combined.

9. Pour the filling into the prepared tart pan and bake for 35 minutes, or until slightly dry on top. Let cool completely on a cooling rack.

Seoul Choco Balls

I can't stress enough how good these are. They are so crunchy and airy, you want to pile 'em in a bowl and drench them in almond milk. Too good to be true.

Makes 24 to 36 cookies

1 ½ cups non-hydrogenated vegan margarine (recommended: Earth Balance)

1 ¼ cups (5.7 ounces) powdered sugar

¼ cup soymilk

1 ½ cups (7.5 ounces) all-purpose flour

1 ¼ cups plus 3 tablespoons (5.7 ounces) almond flour

1 cup (4 ounces) cocoa powder

¼ teaspoon salt

2 ⅔ cups macadamia nuts, finely chopped in a food processor

1. Preheat the oven to 350°F.
2. Line 2 baking sheets with parchment paper.
3. In the bowl of a stand mixer, combine the margarine and sugar, and cream together with the paddle attachment until light and fluffy, 2 to 3 minutes. Scrape the bottom of the bowl and mix again to ensure that all the ingredients are combined, about 30 seconds more.
4. Slowly add the soymilk to the sugar mixture and mix to combine.
5. In a separate bowl, whisk together the flours, cocoa powder, and salt. Stir in the nuts. Add to the sugar mixture and mix until a dough forms.
6. Scoop the dough onto the baking sheets using a spring-loaded ice cream scoop, leaving 2 to 3 inches between each cookie. Use a 2-ounce scoop for larger balls and a 1-ounce scoop for smaller ones.
7. Bake for 15 to 18 minutes, until the cookies look dry. Cool completely on a cooling rack.

Love Bite

....

Macadamia Nuts

Macadamia nuts are, first and foremost, delicious. Second, they are pretty darn good for you, owing to their high levels of fiber and monounsaturated fats—the good fats. Furthermore, one of the fats found in these big guys is palmitoleic acid, which can help break down fats for you to use as energy, making it less likely to store these fats for later. A nut to offset its own fat calories? Yes, please!

Seoul Sugar Balls

These are the Sticky Fingers Seoul version of Mexican wedding cookies. Seoul does a fine job of making tiny little crunchy treats, again, something I want to eat like a bowl of cereal. They are insanely good, and the crunch factor makes them addictive.

Makes 24 to 36 cookies

½ cup non-hydrogenated vegetable shortening (recommended: Earth Balance)

¼ cup non-hydrogenated vegan margarine (recommended: Earth Balance)

¼ cup (1.7 ounces) granulated sugar

3 tablespoons soymilk

½ teaspoon vanilla extract

3 ⅔ cups (1 pounds, 2 ounces) all-purpose flour

½ teaspoon salt

⅔ cup walnuts, finely chopped

1 cup (4.5 ounces) powdered sugar for dusting

1. Preheat the oven to 350°F.
2. Line 2 baking sheets with parchment paper.
3. In the bowl of a stand mixer, combine the shortening, margarine, and granulated sugar and cream together with the paddle attachment until light and fluffy, 2 to 3 minutes. Scrape the bottom of the bowl and mix again to ensure that all the ingredients are combined, about 30 seconds more.
4. Slowly add the soymilk and vanilla to the sugar mixture and mix to combine.
5. In a separate bowl, whisk together the flour and salt. Stir in the walnuts. Add to the sugar mixture and mix until a dough forms.
6. Scoop the dough onto the baking sheets using a tablespoon and roll the dough into small balls. Leave 2 to 3 inches between each cookie.

7. Bake for 10 to 15 minutes, until the cookies look dry.

8. Let the cookies cool on the sheets for 15 to 20 minutes, then place them in a bowl and toss with the powdered sugar.

9. Let the cookies cool completely, then dust with more powdered sugar before serving.

Seoul Sweety Cones

We will admit that we don't understand the "cone" reference here, since these are usually called jam thumbprint cookies in the United States. But "Seoul Sweety Cones" is the translation, so we are sticking to it. And the fact that they are called "sweety" is too endearing, while the deliciousness is too much for words.

Makes 24

1 ¾ cups non-hydrogenated vegan margarine (recommended: Earth Balance)

1 ⅔ cups (11.2 ounces) sugar

1 cup plus 2 tablespoons soymilk

2 ⅔ cups (13.3 ounces) all-purpose flour

1 ¼ cups plus 3 tablespoons (7.5 ounces) cornstarch

1 tablespoon baking powder

1 ½ teaspoons salt

½ cup raspberry jam

1. Preheat the oven to 350ºF.
2. Line 2 baking sheets with parchment paper.
3. In the bowl of a stand mixer, combine the margarine and sugar, and cream together with the paddle attachment until light and fluffy, 2 to 3 minutes. Scrape the bottom of the bowl to ensure that the ingredients are incorporated and mix again, about 1 minute more.
4. Slowly add the soymilk and mix until the ingredients are well combined.
5. In a separate bowl, mix together the all-purpose flour, cornstarch, baking powder, and salt.
6. Add the dry ingredients to the wet ingredients and mix until incorporated.

7. Scoop the dough onto the baking sheets using a 2-ounce spring-loaded ice cream scoop. Leave 2 to 3 inches between each cookie.

8. Using your thumb, press into the top of each cookie lightly to make a little indentation.

9. Scoop a teaspoon of jam into the indentation of each cookie.

10. Bake for 10 to 15 minutes, until the tops look dry.

11. Cool completely on a cooling rack.

Afterword

When this cookbook was first published, we were simply overwhelmed by the response from friends and family, long-time customers, and new fans. We're a tiny little shop and we were so inspired to hear from so many people eager to try their hand at vegan baking. What's more, we were truly honored they wanted to use our recipes in their kitchens. Even more exciting was the interest from mainstream media. We took our demo on the road for morning television programs, national talk shows, and even a radio show or two. People wanted to see (and taste) for themselves if this "vegan thing" was really all that. They needed their own proof that our sweets and treats could actually taste as good, if not better, than the traditional ones they were familiar with.

A few years have passed since our cookbook first hit bookstores, and we've been ridiculously (and happily) busy. We returned to the Food Network's *Cupcake Wars* two more times and (blush) took home the All-Stars win! (We were the first and, to date, are still the only vegans ever to do so, I might add!) Several new recipes came out of that crazy on-air competition that we're excited to share with you.

In our own kitchen, we haven't stopped creating and experimenting, testing and tweaking. With so many ideas and a growing library of recipes for food and drink, we decided to open a second shop—but not a second Sticky Fingers

Sweets & Eats. We launched a new concept that would let us indulge our craving to create new, inventive sweets and also serve "real" food, the perfect complement to our flagship Sticky Fingers. Fare Well serves veggie-centric comfort foods and offerings from a full bakery: fresh breads, savory spreads, hearty soups and stews, casseroles, handmade pastas and sauces, and, of course, a full case of cakes, pastries, and more. At Fare Well, traditional meets new, and the old world gets a fresh twist. Speaking of twists, Fare Well also has a full bar with innovative cocktails and drinks crafted with our house-made syrups.

We look forward to serving you in one of our shops. In the meantime, practice your trade, read the rules, pay attention, and then show us what you've got!

The Rolling Stones:
Brown Sugar Cupcake with Spiced Rum Frosting and Cracked Brown Sugar Brittle

It was an honor to be a part of the Food Network's *Cupcake Wars*, which helped elevate not only Sticky Fingers but also vegan baking. It put our shop—and veganism—on the map.

So when we were asked to return for an All-Stars episode, we jumped at the chance. The days leading up to the competition were like no other. We had won against traditional bakeries and pastry chefs before, but for All-Stars, we were going up against traditional bakeries and pastry chefs who were also all previous winners of *Cupcake Wars*. You can imagine how much we shook and stressed... and how much fun we had!

Our first challenge was to create a cupcake that represented one of the songs on a long list of favorites. As gigantic music nerds, we were so excited! With tunes in our heads, we used our strengths—finding flavors that worked well together to complement and not overpower, and adding a candy technique to accent (and, of course, a little booze for an extra rock 'n' roll kick)—to ensure that we moved on to round two.

Makes 18 cupcakes

2 ¼ cups (11.25 ounces) all-purpose flour

⅜ teaspoon baking soda

⅜ teaspoon salt

1 ¾ cups plus 3 tablespoons (13.5 ounces) lightly packed brown sugar

(continued)

¾ cup non-hydrogenated vegan
   margarine (recommended:
   Earth Balance)
½ cup plus 1 tablespoon water
2 ¼ tablespoons egg replacer
   (recommended: Ener-G)

1 ½ tablespoons vanilla
¾ cup soymilk
¾ teaspoon apple cider vinegar
Spiced Rum Frosting (recipe
   follows)
Brown Sugar Brittle (recipe follows)

1. Preheat the oven to 350°F.
2. Sift the flour, baking soda, and salt into a medium bowl. Set aside.
3. In the bowl of an electric stand mixer, cream the brown sugar and margarine with the whisk attachment, about 5 minutes. Scrape down the sides and bottom of the bowl to ensure the ingredients are incorporated.
4. In a small bowl or cup, combine the water, egg replacer, and vanilla. Stir to dissolve the egg replacer before adding to the sugar. Mix until combined, being sure to scrape the bottom of the bowl. Set aside.
5. In a small bowl, combine the soymilk and vinegar and set aside.
6. Turn the mixer speed to low and slowly add the dry ingredients and the soymilk, alternating between the two, and ending with the soymilk.
7. Fill 18 lined cupcake cups three-quarters full and bake for 16 to 19 minutes, or until a toothpick inserted into each cupcake comes out clean.
8. Place the cupcake tin on a cooling rack to cool completely, then turn the tin upside down to remove the cupcakes.

Spiced Rum Frosting

Makes enough to frost 18 cupcakes

1 cup non-hydrogenated vegetable
    shortening (recommended: Earth
    Balance)

¼ cup plus 2 tablespoons non-
    hydrogenated vegan margarine
    (recommended: Earth Balance)

5 ⅓ cups (1 pound, 8 ounces)
    powdered sugar

1 teaspoon cinnamon

½ teaspoon allspice

¼ teaspoon ground cloves

¼ cup dark rum

1. In the bowl of a stand mixer, combine the shortening and margarine and whip with the paddle attachment until completely combined. Scrape down the sides and bottom of the bowl to ensure that the ingredients are mixed thoroughly.
2. On low speed, slowly add the sugar a little at a time.
3. Add the spices and mix. Scrape the bottom of the bowl.
4. Add the rum and mix to combine. Scrape the bottom of the bowl and mix on medium-high speed until all the ingredients are combined and the frosting is fluffy, about 2 minutes.

Brown Sugar Brittle

1 cup (7 ounces) lightly packed
    brown sugar

½ cup corn syrup

½ teaspoon salt

¼ cup water

1 teaspoon non-hydrogenated vegan
    margarine (recommended: Earth
    Balance)

1 teaspoon baking soda

1. Line a cookie sheet with parchment paper and set aside.

2. In a medium, heavy-bottomed saucepan, combine the sugar, corn syrup, salt, and water. Bring the mixture to a boil over medium-high heat, stirring until the sugar dissolves.

3. Place a candy thermometer into the pan and cook on medium heat, without stirring, until the mixture reaches 300°F.

4. Remove from the heat and quickly stir in the margarine and baking soda.

5. Pour the mixture onto the prepared cookie sheet and quickly spread in a thin layer.

6. Let the candy cool completely and break it into small pieces with your fingers.

7. To assemble: Once the cupcakes have cooled, use a fluted tip in a pastry bag or frost your cupcakes by hand. Garnish with a few pieces of the Brown Sugar Brittle.

The Salt-N-Pepa:
Smoked Black Pepper and Chocolate Cupcake with Vanilla Bean Frosting and Smokey Salted Caramel

Any chance we have to commemorate the genius that is Salt-N-Pepa, we take it. What better way to honor the pair than with a super-hot, sweet, and sassy cupcake!

Makes 18 cupcakes

1 ½ cups plus 1 ½ tablespoons (11.25 ounces) sugar

2 cups (10 ounces) all-purpose flour

½ cup plus 2 tablespoons (2.5 ounces) cocoa powder

2 teaspoons baking soda

2 teaspoons ground smoked black pepper

1 teaspoon salt

1 ⅜ cups water

¼ cup coffee, room temperature

½ cup plus 1 tablespoon vegetable or canola oil

½ tablespoon vanilla

2 tablespoons apple cider vinegar

Vanilla Bean Frosting (recipe follows)

Caramel Sauce (recipe follows)

Smoked salt, for garnish

1. Preheat the oven to 350°F.
2. Sift the sugar, flour, cocoa, baking soda, smoked black pepper, and salt into a medium bowl and set aside.
3. In a small bowl, whisk together the water, coffee, oil, and vanilla.
4. Add the wet ingredients to the dry ingredients and whisk until just incorporated.

5. Add the vinegar and incorporate. Do not overmix the batter.

6. Fill 18 lined cupcake cups three-quarters full and bake for 16 to 19 minutes, or until a toothpick inserted into each cupcake comes out clean.

7. Place the cupcake tins on a cooling rack to cool completely, then turn the tins upside down to remove the cupcakes.

Vanilla Bean Frosting

Makes enough to frost 18 cupcakes

1 cup non-hydrogenated vegetable shortening (recommended: Earth Balance)

¼ cup plus 2 tablespoons non-hydrogenated vegan margarine (recommended: Earth Balance)

6 ¼ cups (1 pound, 12 ounces) powdered sugar

Seeds from 2 vanilla beans or 3 teaspoons vanilla bean paste

⅓ to ½ cup soymilk, as needed

1. In the bowl of an electric stand mixer, combine the shortening and margarine and whip with the paddle attachment until completely combined. Scrape the sides and bottom of the bowl to ensure that the ingredients are mixed thoroughly.

2. On low speed, slowly add the sugar a little at a time.

3. Once the sugar is incorporated, add the vanilla bean seeds and soymilk and mix on low until the liquids are incorporated.

4. Scrape the sides and bottom of the bowl and mix on medium-high speed until all the ingredients are combined and the frosting is fluffy, about 2 minutes.

Caramel Sauce

Makes about 2 cups

2 cups (14 ounces) sugar

2 tablespoons corn syrup

½ cup water

⅔ cup soy creamer or canned coconut milk

Pinch of salt

2 teaspoons non-hydrogenated vegan margarine (recommended: Earth Balance)

1 teaspoon smoked or flake salt

[handwritten note: Overcooked. do want this full 20 min]

1. In a small, heavy-bottomed saucepan, stir together the sugar, corn syrup, and water over medium-high heat. Cover and bring to a boil.

2. Let the mixture boil, without stirring, until it starts to turn brown, about 20 minutes. Remove from the heat and stir with a whisk. *[handwritten circle around "20 minutes"]*

3. Quickly add the creamer and salt and carefully continue stirring. Once the bubbling stops, add the margarine and whisk until it is melted and distributed.

4. Let the sauce cool completely before pouring into a clean squirt bottle or pastry bag.

5. To assemble: Once the cupcakes have cooled, use a fluted tip in a pastry bag or frost your cupcakes by hand. Drizzle the top with Caramel Sauce and sprinkle with smoked or flake salt to garnish.

The Chuck Berry: Orange Cupcake with Blueberry Filling and Raspberry Frosting

Pushing the limits. Taking a taste and running with it. Hints of country, a touch of tart, zesty sweet, and happy-dance-inducing. Meet the "Chuck Berry."

Makes 18 cupcakes

2 ½ cups plus 2 tablespoons (13 ounces) all-purpose flour

1 tablespoon baking powder

½ teaspoon salt

⅛ teaspoon xanthan gum

1 ¼ cups plus 3 tablespoons (10 ounces) sugar

½ cup plus 2 tablespoons non-hydrogenated vegan margarine (recommended: Earth Balance)

¼ cup water

2 teaspoons egg replacer (recommended: Ener-G)

1 ½ cups plus 2 tablespoons soymilk

1 ½ teaspoons vanilla

Zest from 1 orange

⅛ teaspoon orange oil

Blueberry Filling (recipe follows)

Raspberry Frosting (recipe follows)

Fresh blueberries and/or raspberries, for garnish (optional)

1. Preheat the oven to 350°F.
2. Sift the flour, baking powder, salt, and xanthan gum into a medium bowl and set aside.
3. In the bowl of an electric stand mixer, cream together the sugar and the margarine with the whisk attachment, about 5 minutes. Scrape down the sides and bottom of the bowl.

4. In a small bowl or cup, combine the water and egg replacer. Stir to dissolve the egg replacer before adding to the sugar. Mix until combined.

5. In a small bowl, combine the soymilk, vanilla, orange zest, and orange oil and set aside.

6. Turn the mixer speed to low and slowly add the dry ingredients and the soymilk mixture, alternating between the two, ending with the soymilk mixture.

7. Fill 18 lined cupcake cups three-quarters full and bake for 16 to 19 minutes, or until a toothpick inserted into each cupcake comes out clean.

8. Place the cupcake tins on a cooling rack to cool completely, then turn the tins upside down to remove the cupcakes.

Blueberry Filling

Makes about 2 cups

2 cups blueberries, fresh or frozen
1/4 cup (1.75 ounces) sugar
2 tablespoons cornstarch
1/2 teaspoon cinnamon
1/2 cup port wine

1. In a medium, heavy-bottomed saucepan, stir together the blueberries, sugar, cornstarch, cinnamon, and port. Heat on medium-high until the mixture begins to bubble around the edges.

2. Cook until the mixture begins to thicken, 10 to 15 minutes.

3. Remove from the heat and let the filling cool completely.

Raspberry Frosting

Makes enough to frost 18 cupcakes

1 cup plus 2 tablespoons non-hydrogenated vegetable shortening (recommended: Earth Balance)

¼ cup plus 2 tablespoons non-hydrogenated vegan margarine (recommended: Earth Balance)

⅓ cup raspberry puree, store-bought or homemade (see Note, page 40)

4 ¼ cups (1 pound, 3 ounces) powdered sugar

1 ½ tablespoons lemon juice

1. In the bowl of an electric stand mixer, combine the shortening and margarine and whip with the paddle attachment until completely combined. Scrape the sides and bottom of the bowl to ensure that the ingredients are mixed thoroughly.
2. On low speed, add the raspberry puree and mix until incorporated.
3. Scrape the sides and bottom of the bowl, and slowly add the sugar a little at a time.
4. Add the lemon juice and mix to combine. Scrape the sides and bottom of the bowl, and mix on medium-high speed until all the ingredients are combined and the frosting is fluffy, about 2 minutes.
5. To assemble: Once the cupcakes have cooled, cut holes in the center of each cupcake, using a spoon or knife. Using a piping bag or spoon, fill the center with about 1 tablespoon of the puree. Use a round tip in a pastry bag or frost the top of your cupcakes by hand. Pretty it up with a fresh blueberry or raspberry on top, if you like.

The Man in Black (aka Johnny Cash):
Black Chocolate Cupcake with Toasted Cashews, Black Chocolate Frosting, Spun Sugar Hay, and Cashew Chocolate Boots

We've been looking for an excuse to use black cocoa for a while, which we encountered by accident when we were delivered the wrong cocoa in an order. It turned out to be so right. This cocoa makes your chocolatiest of cakes even richer, and the frosting's music to your mouth. You'll dig our homage to Johnny Cash-ew....

Makes 18 cupcakes

1 ½ cups plus 1 ½ tablespoons (11.25 ounces) sugar

2 cups (10 ounces) all-purpose flour

½ cup plus 2 tablespoons (2.5 ounces) black cocoa powder

2 teaspoons baking soda

¾ teaspoon salt

1 ³/₈ cups water

¼ cup strong-brewed coffee, cooled

½ cup plus 1 tablespoon vegetable or canola oil

½ tablespoon vanilla

2 tablespoons apple cider vinegar

1 cup chopped unsalted cashews, toasted

Black Chocolate Frosting (recipe follows)

Spun Sugar Hay Bale (recipe follows)

Cashew Chocolate Cowboy Boots (recipe follows)

1. Preheat the oven to 350°F.
2. Sift the sugar, flour, cocoa, baking soda, and salt into a medium bowl and set aside.
3. In a small bowl, whisk together the water, coffee, oil, and vanilla.
4. Add the wet ingredients to the dry ingredients and whisk until just incorporated.
5. Add the vinegar and incorporate, taking care not to overmix the batter.
6. Fill 18 lined cupcake cups three-quarters full and sprinkle 1 tablespoon of toasted cashews on top of each cupcake. Bake for 16 to 19 minutes, or until a toothpick inserted into each cupcake comes out clean.
7. Place the cupcake tins on a cooling rack to cool completely, then turn the tins upside down to remove the cupcakes.

Black Chocolate Frosting

Makes enough to frost 18 cupcakes

1 cup non-hydrogenated vegetable shortening (recommended: Earth Balance)

¼ cup plus 2 tablespoons non-hydrogenated vegan margarine (recommended: Earth Balance)

4 ½ cups (1 pound, 4 ounces) powdered sugar

½ cup (2 ounces) black cocoa powder

6 ounces dark chocolate, melted and slightly cooled

½ cup soymilk

1. In the bowl of an electric stand mixer, combine the shortening and margarine and whip with the paddle attachment until combined. Scrape the sides and bottom of the bowl to ensure that the ingredients are mixed thoroughly.
2. On low speed, slowly add the sugar and cocoa powder a little at a time. Scrape the sides and bottom of the bowl.

3. Once the sugar and cocoa are incorporated, add the melted chocolate and soymilk and mix on low speed until combined.

4. Scrape the sides and bottom of the bowl and mix on medium-high speed until all the ingredients are combined and the frosting is fluffy, about 2 minutes.

Spun Sugar Hay Bale

½ cup (3.5 ounces) sugar
⅓ cup corn syrup

1. Prepare your work station: Cover your kitchen counter and floor with newspaper to catch sugar spills.

2. Take 3 or 4 saucepans and arrange them close together on the paper-covered counter, handles facing outward and extending over the edge of the counter. Spray the handles with nonstick cooking spray.

3. Fill a large bowl with ice and water and set it aside.

4. Combine the sugar and corn syrup in a medium saucepan over medium-high heat and stir until the sugar dissolves.

5. Cover the saucepan with a lid and boil for 2 to 3 minutes, then remove the lid and continue to boil the sugar syrup, stirring occasionally, until it reaches 310°F on a candy thermometer or just begins to get golden. The sugar will cook very quickly toward the end, so watch closely to ensure it doesn't burn.

6. As soon as the sugar reaches the proper temperature, remove the saucepan from the heat and dunk the bottom into the prepared ice water to stop the sugar from cooking further. Allow the mixture to stand for 1 or 2 minutes to thicken slightly. Remove the saucepan from the ice water bath.

7. Use a fork (or a whisk that has been cut open) to stir the sugar. Remove the fork from the pot and let it drizzle off for a second or two. Hold it 5 to 6 inches above the prepared saucepan handles and rapidly flick the

fork back and forth over the handles. The sugar syrup should create very fine strands of sugar that drape over the handles. If the syrup doesn't create any strands, or the strands have a lot of beads, allow the syrup to cool for another minute. If the strands are lumpy and difficult to form, reheat the syrup very briefly.

8. Continue to dip and quickly flick the fork over the handles, creating many fine strands of spun sugar. Remove the sugar strands from the handle. Wrap the strands into a small "hay bale" and set aside. Continue to create spun sugar until your syrup is gone, or until you have enough hay bales for all the cupcakes.

Cashew Chocolate Cowboy Boots

8 ounces dark chocolate, chopped
½ cup chopped unsalted cashews, toasted

1. Set a heatproof bowl over a pan of simmering water. Place the chocolate in the bowl and stir occasionally, until melted.
2. Remove from the heat and stir in the toasted cashews. Spoon the melted chocolate into cowboy boot-shaped chocolate candy molds and place in the refrigerator for 15 minutes until the chocolate sets.
3. Remove from the molds and place the candies on parchment paper until ready to use.
4. To assemble: Once your cupcakes have cooled, use a fluted tip in a pastry bag or frost your cupcakes by hand. Place a Spun Sugar Hay bale on top of each cupcake and garnish with a Cashew Chocolate Cowboy Boot.

Acknowledgments

Special love and thank-you to Kamber Sherrod, Paul Petersan, Ben Adams, Jenny Webb, the Sticky Fingers staff, Team Sticky Fingers, Kirsten Rosenberg, Lucia Watson, Laura Dail, Rory Freedman, and all of the devoted customers who were inadvertently our blind taste-testers.

To all of those who helped test small batches in their very own kitchens;

Deidre Franklin

Jeff Bearington

Candace and Jack Ryan

Matt Prescott

Lara Sanders

Laura Casperson

Scott Fulton

Rebecca Cary

Acknowledgments

Danielle Bays

Carol Casperson

Kate Stephens

Lori Bays

Rachel Wehlburg

Christine Fuentes

Kristen Monsell

Nancy Perry

Aimee Gogan

Tessa Hale

Tina and Brad Conway

Katie Shamp

Brian Knaack

Karla Goodson

Jessica Berry

Index